Awakenings from the Light

Awakenings from the Light

12 LIFE LESSONS FROM A NEAR DEATH EXPERIENCE

―⊖⊖⊖―

Nancy Rynes

Copyright (c) 2015 Nancy Rynes (NancyRynes.com)

Published and distributed in the United States by: CreateSpace and Amazon.com, in cooperation with Solace Press (Denver, CO)

Project Editor: Amy Collette Casey
Author Photo: Ashley Deaner Photography, LLC.

All rights reserved. No part of this book may be reproduced by any means; nor may it be stored in a retrieval system, transmitted, or otherwise copied for public or private use — other than "fair use" as short quotations in articles or reviews — without prior written permission of the author.

The author of this book does not dispense any medical or psychological advice, or prescribe the use of any technique as a form of treatment for physical, medical, emotional, or mental health problems without the advice of a physician or other trained professional, either directly or indirectly. The intent of the author is only to offer information from her own experience, and of a general nature to help you in your quest for spiritual understanding and well-being. In the event you use any of the information in this book for yourself, which is your right, the author assumes no responsibility for your actions.

If you are experiencing physical, medical, emotional, or spiritual issues, the author advises you to seek the advice of an appropriate professional (medical doctor, psychotherapist, counselor, etc.).

Library of Congress Cataloging-in-Publication Data

Rynes, Nancy
Awakenings from the Light — Lessons on Life from a Near-Death Experience
ISBN: 1508453748
ISBN 13: 9781508453741
Library of Congress Control Number: 2015903706
CreateSpace Independent Publishing Platform
North Charleston, South Carolina

First edition, May 2015

Printed in the United States of America

This book is dedicated to the Lafayette, Colorado, Police and Fire Departments, and to first responders everywhere. You rock!

Table of Contents

Foreword · ix
Acknowledgements · xi
Author's Note · xv
Introduction · xix
Part One – Changes · 1
Chapter 1   In An Instant… · 3
Chapter 2   Surgery · 18
Chapter 3   Another World · 22
Chapter 4   My Guide · 26
Part Two – Messages from Spirit · · · · · · · · · · · · · · · 39
Chapter 5   The Messages · 41
Chapter 6   Love and Compassion · · · · · · · · · · · · · · · · 49
Chapter 7   You Are A Miracle · · · · · · · · · · · · · · · · · · · 70
Chapter 8   Earth is a Miracle · · · · · · · · · · · · · · · · · · · 80
Chapter 9   We Are Creative and Powerful · · · · · · · · · · 88
Chapter 10   We Are All Connected · · · · · · · · · · · · · · · · 99
Chapter 11   Allow, Let Go · 105
Chapter 12   Allow Others to Show Love · · · · · · · · · · · 119
Chapter 13   Listen to Your Inner Wisdom · · · · · · · · · · 125
Chapter 14   We Are Never Alone · · · · · · · · · · · · · · · · 138
Chapter 15   Choice · 151
Chapter 16   Live Your Life Fully · · · · · · · · · · · · · · · · · 164
Chapter 17   Gratitude · 176

	Part Three – Recovering	189
Chapter 18	Body and Mind	191
Chapter 19	My Life Changes	207
Chapter 20	A New Job	211
Chapter 21	Why Me?	215
Chapter 22	What's in it for You?	217
Chapter 23	In Closing	220
	Part Four – Appendices	223
Chapter 24	A) What Did Death Feel Like?	225
Chapter 25	B) The Others	228
Chapter 26	C) Reading List	230
	About the Author	231
	Nancy's Programs	233

Foreword

I BELIEVE I WAS LEAD to Nancy's room in the Intensive Care unit that January day of 2014. In my duties as the hospital's chaplain, I just wanted to stop by and greet this new patient. It did not take long to realize that this would not be a quick visit as planned. As I sat down, I soon realized that this person had gone through a major earthquake-like transformation in her life and was now struggling to simply find the words to describe it.

Not only was Nancy's body broken in numerous pieces, but her heart was also broken open, and new life was streaming from it so powerfully that it overwhelmed even her. Nancy had just experienced a taste of life after death, and the door to Divine influence that had been locked for years had now flung open without her choosing. The experience of God's powerful love had melted away all resistance like the spring sun melts the most hardened ice. So, we sat there and marveled at it all.

It was like Henri Nouwen in his book *Life of the Beloved* said after a beautiful crystal challis crashed onto the floor and splintered into thousands of pieces: he never knew that broken glass could shine so brightly. That described Nancy's brokenness. She had wanted a life change, but it was not planned this way. It is amazing how the things we would never have chosen for ourselves can be the most powerful agents of change.

In her book, Nancy leads us into her life and heart-changing experience of being in "pre-Heaven," accompanied by a Guide. Upon returning into her body, Nancy remains vulnerable and bravely continues to unwrap this gift to share with us her newfound wisdom.

She is a Pilgrim who has traveled into a death, beyond it, and back, and brings to us the treasure of her pilgrimage. She humbly acknowledges that in many ways it is only the start of a faith journey, and there is still so much to be discovered.

Come and be a pilgrim with her!

Her Caregiver and fellow Pilgrim,

Rev. Liena Apsukrapsa

Acknowledgements

It takes a village to write a book, and this book certainly needed a large village. I am deeply grateful for the gathering of souls who helped make this book what it is:

First and foremost, my deepest gratitude to Spirit for my life, for love, and for the opportunity to serve. And thank you for giving me this second chance.

I'm also deeply grateful to my Guide, the spiritual being who accompanied me on my trip through Heaven. Thank you for being both a messenger and an ongoing source of inspiration.

Thank you to my parents for the gift of life.

My deepest thanks go to the many people who worked selflessly to save my life after my accident: the Lafayette Colorado Fire and Police Departments; the witnesses at the scene who stopped to help; Ann, the trauma nurse who saved my ability to walk; the trauma and emergency room teams at Good Samaritan Hospital; the many physicians, chaplains, physician assistants, nurses, therapists, CNAs, and technicians who cared for me; and all of the staff at the hospital who tried to make my stay as comfortable as possible.

I'm grateful to Angela Molitoris and Ellen McWethy for holding my hands and keeping me company in the hours before my surgery.

A heartfelt "Thank you" goes to the staff at Exelis VIS in Boulder, Colorado, who supported me so beautifully in the weeks and months after my recovery.

Thank you to Scott Lekrone and Ken Elliott for gently encouraging me to write this book, and to CJ Wells for scheduling my first public talk about my experience. Thank you to Jacqueline Arnold for lending your loving support and encouragement when I very much needed it.

I'm deeply indebted to Amy Collette Casey, my friend and editor, for: supporting me in my recovery, the many talks about Spirit, and for her expert work editing this book. Amy's keen eye and superior word-smithing skills turned my "just OK" manuscript into something truly readable.

Thank you to the people who read the manuscript and gave me thoughts and insights: Eric Brown, Lisa Meserve, Alison Dombek, Sara Beth Brown, Tom Tindell, Ron Iverson, Mearl Halsall, and John Crandall. I very much appreciate your input!

To my social media friends and followers who continue to encourage and inspire me. You're all gems!

My deepest thanks to Rev. Liena Apsukrapsa, chaplain at Good Samaritan Hospital, for listening, and for caring so much about the patients she serves.

I'm grateful to my primary care physician for supporting my health and recovery so beautifully, and for believing me when I told him about my NDE.

A huge "Thank you" goes to those friends who were there for me through this process: Ashley and Justin Deaner, Alison Dombek, Amy Casey, Derek Stoddard, Nicole and Wes Hyde, Debra and Eldon Warren, Tom Tindell, Don Barnes, John Crandall, and many others.

I'm grateful for the beautiful presence of my daughter in my life. Cara, you truly are a blessing.

No amount of words are enough to thank my family members and friends who stepped in and made my recovery possible. Chrissy and Mike Debruine, my niece and her husband, for being there for me when I needed them. And thanks to Evalyn's presence for brightening my day whenever she walked in the room. Special thanks to my dear friend, Marilyn Ryan, for her unflagging support over the last 18 years. I'm especially in her debt, though, for coming here to Colorado to help me recover from my accident. Thanks to my sisters, Jennifer Kovacik and Mary Jo Colligan, and their husbands Greg and Glenn, for dropping everything to come out here to help me heal.

You are all blessings, and I am lucky to have you in my life.

Author's Note

One of the difficulties I faced when writing this book was deciding on the terminology. So many of the words we use to describe spirituality or spiritual concepts are loaded with emotion or tied to a particular belief system.

After my near-death experience (NDE), my own beliefs have come to encompass ideas from many faiths, even though I align more with what I call an open-hearted Christianity or spirituality. I now understand that a similar core of beauty and truth lies at the heart of many of our religions and philosophies, so in my own life, I embrace the loving wisdom from different faiths. When I began to write this book, it made sense that I wanted to use words that were meaningful *across* faiths, rather than exclusive to one.

That proved to be a bigger challenge than I expected. I struggled with finding a term to use to describe a Higher Power, one that would be inclusive of many faiths. In the end, I chose to use "Spirit" as much as possible. This word seems to best describe the sense of mystery that I feel about what some might call "God." In my own mind, I don't look upon the concept of Spirit or God as a person (i.e., of human form) sitting on a cloud somewhere, passing judgment. Spirit is a mystery, something that really can't be described adequately with a word or a phrase. But the word "Spirit" is a start. I also use the words "God," "Divine," and "Creator," interchangeably, as a name for that mysterious Higher Power.

I hope the different words aren't too confusing, and I invite you to substitute the word that feels most comfortable for you.

Similarly, I had many long discussions with friends about how to refer to the spiritual being I met during my near-death experience. Some wanted me to use the term "angel," but I felt that wasn't quite right, especially since she didn't refer to herself in that way. In the end, I decided to use the term "Guide," as suggested by a fellow artist and friend, Ken Elliott. It's simple, clear, and easy to understand.

The word "Heaven" also proved challenging. As a child in the Roman Catholic faith, the priests taught me that Heaven was a separate place, up in the sky, where the souls of "good" people went after death. While my view of what happens after life has changed a lot in the last 15+ months, I still couldn't come up with a meaningful term to replace "Heaven." I decided to simply go ahead and use it, knowing that, in my mind, it's not exactly the right word. I don't use it in the traditional, Christian sense, though, meaning it's not some *place* up on a cloud that we go when we die. For the purposes of my story, "Heaven" simply refers to that very mysterious state of being, or realm, that I found myself in. It might indeed be a place, although the sense that I got while there is that Heaven is more truly a shift in state or energy from our physical plane.

I don't intend to wrap the meaning of the word "Heaven" in any particular religion or philosophy. Feel free to put your own word in its place. For myself, I am content leaving it to the realm of deep mystery.

At a few points in the book, I felt it necessary to include the actual words given to me by my Guide, and they're set apart from the rest of the text. Similarly, in a few places, I wanted to include appropriate thoughts or quotes from other, learned people that seem to emphasize a particular concept. While I've tried to include thoughts from a variety of cultures, you might notice that I lean heavily on Native American wisdom at times. I have a little Native American ancestry in my background, so some of this wisdom resonates with me.

Please also note that I'm not a counselor, physician, or religious leader. If you have emotional or mental challenges, are being treated for a mental illness, or are in distress, I urge you to seek the advice of a trained professional for help.

I'll finish with a note about photos. Many of my friends wanted me to include photos of the accident and my recovery in this book. The realities of publishing made that financially out of reach for this first edition. I have posted photos on this book's website, *AwakeningsFromTheLight.com*, if you're interested in visuals. The link to photos is in the upper-right corner of the home screen.

Introduction

My life was pretty quiet during the autumn of 2013. As summer wound down, I spent a bit more time indoors and a little less outside riding one of my bicycles. The fewer hours of daylight that autumn brings made it tough to get out on after-work rides, which meant more hours in the gym and fewer out on the roads. But autumn and winter always gave me a chance to spend more time pursuing my primary passion — oil painting — so in a way, I looked forward to the change in season.

My professional life hadn't changed much from previous years. Being a technical writer was manageable for me: not terribly stressful, yet challenging. I liked my coworkers and enjoyed going in to the office. But after almost 20 years working similar jobs in the science and technology industries, I wondered if I might need a change in this part of my life.

My romantic life was at a low point, too. Yet another potential relationship had evaporated in early October. I knew it was in my best interests to break things off with this man but the ending still rattled me and cast a pall over the ensuing weeks. And like many singles, I didn't much enjoy the prospect of going in to another holiday season alone.

In my past, the darker days of November signaled a temporary downshift in my mood, and 2013 was no different. The fewer hours of daylight, coupled with anniversaries of the deaths of several close family members, usually cast a somber note over this month for me. This year I felt an additional layer of unease. In hindsight, I think I was starting to realize that my life wasn't feeling *right* to me in some way, even though I couldn't pinpoint exactly what was wrong. I felt uncomfortable in my own skin, that I was on the wrong path somehow, and out of alignment with who I was.

I didn't really know what to do about my uneasy feelings, so I let them slide and just soldiered on.

I was good at soldiering on. "Keep marching ahead and don't complain," was my mantra for most of that November.

Things started to change for me just days before Thanksgiving. November 25, almost 12 years to the day that my eldest sister died in a terrible car accident, a distracted driver rear-ended my vehicle while I was stopped at a traffic light. I had no room to get out of his way as his luxury car crashed into the back of my small SUV. The crash totaled my car, but luckily I came away with only minor injuries.

Even though fortune was on my side that day, something about this accident got under my skin. The driver lied about what happened — he told me one story about losing control of his car, but told the police something completely different. He was a prominent professional in our community, yet seemed unconcerned about me or the changes that he brought into my life.

I needed to replace my vehicle but realized that getting another one would put a dent in my monthly bottom line. Because my car was older, his insurance company paid out very little on the claim. In my Pollyanna mind, I hoped that he would step up to the plate, take responsibility for causing the crash, and replace my damaged car himself.

Things don't often work out the way we'd like.

I ended up footing the bill for another vehicle myself without even a basic apology from the other driver or his insurance company.

The accident and its aftermath left me restless, angry, and looking for *something* to change in my life. But I couldn't quite figure out what that *something* was.

Early December came and with it, bizarre dreams that kept me from sleeping soundly. These dreams were very strange, colorful, beautiful, and yet disturbing in some way that I didn't understand. My sisters and a few friends thought they had mystical significance, but with my background as a scientist and my career in technology, I wasn't quite open to those types of explanations. I was on the fence about God, spirituality, and an afterlife. I didn't really believe in the God of my Roman Catholic upbringing and nothing since then had felt right to me. I wanted to believe in something greater than simply physical reality, but never really saw any evidence of it.

But while speaking with my sisters and friends during the month of December, I did have strong feelings from deep inside my being that my life was about to change, and drastically. I verbalized this to my sisters and friends, but none of us had a clue as to what it meant or what to do about it.

A week or so later I heard Sara Barielles' song *December* for the first time. It's a beautiful and haunting song, but there was one line in particular that really grabbed me. Sara sung about the need to give up your old life if you wanted a new life to come your way. Something clicked in my consciousness. I started thinking that if I wanted to make positive changes in my life, I'd need to let go of the things that weren't working so well for me.

As I replayed those lyrics and contemplated their wisdom, I had yet another sense that parts of my old life were about to die and new ones would be filling in the gaps. I'd have to give up old patterns and old ways of thinking. I had no idea what my new life would be, though. I assumed it involved getting a different job, or perhaps finding more friends or a new romance. All were within the realm of possibility for me, but I didn't actively seek them out, either.

I called a longtime friend and told her about these feelings and the dreams. She didn't offer any insights but she thought the best course was just to wait and trust that things would get clearer with time.

A few weeks later, my whole life flipped upside down. A simple bike ride to run some errands led to almost everything in my life changing in a heartbeat. The most profound change was my outlook on matters of Spirit.

PART ONE

Changes

CHAPTER 1

In An Instant...

JANUARY ALONG THE COLORADO FRONT Range can be a beautiful thing.

After the frigid days of December, Mother Nature usually gifts us with abundant warmth and sunshine in the first month of the New Year. On some days, the temperature reaches 70 degrees Fahrenheit and the first wispy scents of spring meander on the breeze.

January 3, 2014, brought in sunshine and warm breezes. By 10:30 AM the temperature neared 60 degrees Fahrenheit, the sun shone bright and warm, and the dry roads beckoned me out on my bicycle. The colder weather and some injuries from the car accident around Thanksgiving had kept me cooped up for much of December. I felt strong and more than ready to hit the roads. A longtime road cyclist, I appreciated being able to ride outside all year here in the Rocky Mountain State, so a month off the bike was almost impossible for me to handle.

Road cycling was my passion. I loved its speed and rhythm, often riding 30-40 miles several times a week. I rode for hours on the plains and challenged myself on the hills — and this is Colorado, so I had plenty of hills to choose from.

Since the day was just about perfect I decided to run some errands around town on my mountain bike. I thought that since it was more stable and had wider tires, the mountain bike would perform better if I ran into any sand or dirt on the road. The other reason I chose my mountain bike was that this was my first ride in over a month and I wanted its stability and more upright posture in case I had lost some of my cycling mojo. Balance is key on any bike, but even more of an issue with the skinny, slick tires of my road bike than the fat, rugged treads of my mountain bike. And since I was a little out of shape from the previous month off, I planned a slower, shorter outing than usual. The slower ride would also allow me to bask longer in the warm, winter sunlight.

The ride started out promising enough. I intended to go out for a quick and easy jaunt south out of town toward the hospital, then stop at some stores, the library, and the post office before calling it a day. I rolled my mountain bike out of the garage, put air in the tires, cleaned the chain, and donned my cool weather clothes and helmet. In what turned out to be a lucky happenstance, I filled up my backpack with clothing in case it was cooler than I thought. The sun felt warm as I prepared my bike but I knew that I might feel colder once I got out on the open roads.

When the bike was ready, I rode south from my home for about 1/2 mile. I felt physically strong, alert, and glad there was very little traffic. My legs felt good getting back into the cadence of pedaling again. I reveled in the feeling of my leg muscles pushing the pedals.

At just shy of a mile from my starting point, I cautiously rode into the new roundabout that recently replaced a three-way intersection. No one in town that I'd spoken with liked the roundabout – the lanes were very narrow, the turns were very tight, and the concrete dividers made navigation difficult. It was difficult enough to drive through it in a car, so I used extra caution as I rode into it on my bike.

Once in the roundabout, I continued riding south in the bike lane. A small car followed me into the circle but stayed a couple of car lengths behind me. I kept my eyes on some vehicles approaching on the road to the right, but I didn't worry too much since they appeared to be slowing down to yield to traffic already in the circle.

As I began to cross in front of the incoming traffic, it appeared that the driver of the lead vehicle, a very large SUV, saw me and was stopping. A split second later, though, I realized she was driving straight into the circle without even slowing down.

Panic gripped me and knotted in my gut. I knew without a doubt I was going to be hit and thought I would likely die. The odds of a cyclist coming out alive in a confrontation with an SUV were pretty low.

Thoughts of my daughter, sisters, and niece flashed through my mind. In a split second I realized how devastated they might be when they found out I had died. I wouldn't witness my daughter grow into the amazing woman I knew she would be. I wouldn't see my niece marry the man of her dreams, or her daughter grow into a beautiful woman. I regretted that my sisters would be grieving over me. Losing another sister in our family would not be easy for them to endure.

I tried to steer my bike to avoid a crash but I couldn't get out of the SUV's way fast enough. The roundabout was narrow and while I started to veer to my left to avoid a crash, I didn't have much room to maneuver. I remembered the car behind me and I didn't want to do anything that would cause it to hit me as well. I felt trapped.

The SUV continued into the circle as if the driver didn't see me. The worst thing I could imagine, happened. The SUV hit me broadside, from the right, impacting my right leg and ribcage. As it did, I tried to push off it with my right hand hoping to propel myself out of the way of its tires. It didn't work. I felt my bike slipping away from under me and knew I was going down. In a flash of odd clarity I figured that was it, I would die right there. Thoughts of my family and friends again went through my mind. Oddly, though, I didn't feel any physical pain.

Somehow I ended up on the SUV's hood. I remember looking through the windshield to the driver and passengers before slipping further down the hood. It appeared that the driver was holding a cell phone in front of her on her steering wheel, but I couldn't be sure with the brief glance I had of her.[1] Up on the hood, I couldn't find anything to grab so I began to slip down the front of the SUV. Without understanding how I got there, I soon found myself clinging to the front grille

---

[1] Witness accounts verified that the driver of the SUV appeared to be texting for the several hundred yards before she hit me. While she was initially charged for this offense, plus three others, the District Attorney's office dropped the texting charge due to difficulties in obtaining enough proof to convict.

of the truck, hoping against hope that I wouldn't get pulled under the vehicle. Time seemed suspended. I felt as though I clung to the grille for hours. In reality, though, only seconds passed.

I didn't know what had happened to my bike. I assumed by now that it was under the truck's rear wheels. I had no idea why I wasn't there too.

Still the truck continued to drive — it didn't stop when it hit me or when I was up on its hood.

After what seemed like forever but was probably only a few more seconds, I lost my grip on the SUV's grille and have a clear memory of grasping at the license plate, hoping again that I wouldn't be pulled under, terrified that I *would* be pulled under. I was in animal survival mode, doing anything possible to hold on and stay alive.

Exactly what I feared would happen, did. I lost my grip on the license plate.

In another second I was under the SUV, my helmeted head and left shoulder hitting the pavement with a pair of loud cracks. Oddly enough, though, I don't remember feeling any pain through this. I felt no pain at the initial impact with the truck and still felt no pain as I struck the pavement.

But I did feel fear deep in the pit of my stomach.

The terror that I would be run over almost paralyzed me. By a stroke of luck I somehow retained consciousness. Why I didn't black out, I still don't know. Now, several months later and after speaking with my doctors, I am more convinced that the blow to my head should have knocked me out cold even with my helmet on. Most people in this situation would have lost consciousness but if I had, there is no doubt I would have died. The vehicle's rear wheels would have run over me. While remaining conscious turned out to be a terrifying experience that would later cause me some post-traumatic stress, it turned out to have been a blessing. Staying conscious saved my life.

As the SUV pulled me under, my sternum caught on its transfer case at the same time that I reached up and grabbed the axle with my right arm. Again, I was doing anything possible to hang on. I have no memory of *knowing* that I needed to grab something. My instincts simply told me to find something to grab and the axle was mercifully within my reach.

The SUV still moved and dragged me with it, my body pinned between the transfer case and the asphalt. My backpack, hips, legs, and shoes made direct contact with the road's surface for approximately 50 feet. My pack and shoes even left a long skid mark that police would later use to determine the speed of the SUV and the duration of the accident.[2]

In those moments under the SUV, I whimpered like a hurt animal with only thoughts of survival in my mind, and the need to stay away from the deadly rear tires. Oddly, my memory flashed back 27 years to a raccoon I accidentally struck and killed while driving home from college one night. I now had a small glimpse into the terror that little animal probably felt in its last moments. Empathy, sadness, and remorse overwhelmed me as the SUV continued to drag me under it.

Then I noticed something very odd. At that moment I realized my consciousness was in two places at once.

I didn't think much about it at the time except "Wow, that's weird." But later, even today, I still find it difficult to wrap my brain and emotions around that experience of dual-consciousness. My training as a scientist couldn't provide an explanation for this, but the experience stuck in my memory.

It seemed like the animal or survival-focused part of my consciousness stayed under the truck in my body, hanging on to the axle, whimpering, and trying not to get run over. That part was all about fear, raw emotion, and survival. *But another part of my consciousness watched the whole accident unfold from out in front and to the side of the SUV!* How could this be?

The displaced and "observer-me" was oddly dispassionate about what unfolded. While it was definitely me, this part of my consciousness did not feel any panic or fear. She maintained an oddly calm state of being, thoughtful yet loving. She felt she was witnessing something sad but also something that was supposed to happen just the way it was unfolding. I

---

[2] A few hours later, I would be grateful that I had stuffed my backpack with clothing. While in the ER later that day, the trauma team would point out to me that the pack had protected the skin on my back from being shredded during the time that I was being dragged under the SUV.

distinctly remember that this observer-me felt everything would be OK, so why be frightened?

My observer consciousness saw the front of the truck, read the license plate, saw the driver inside, the people from other vehicles stopping to help and intervene, and eventually it saw the SUV stop.

I had this dual sense of consciousness for what seemed like hours but in reality was only a few minutes. Being in two places was an odd state of being and one I had no experience with.[3]

It turned out that after the initial impact, the driver dragged me for approximately 50 feet under the vehicle. In those few minutes while I laid under the truck and before the paramedics arrived, the animal part of me wanted to get up and run away as fast as possible. I guess that's not an uncommon survival instinct, but in my case it would have done me more harm than good.

But my animal-mind didn't know that. When I thought it was safe, I tried to squirm out from under the axle. My fear screamed at me to get up and run as far away as I could. All the while, the observer-me simply watched and waited.

When I began my struggle to move, searing pain ripped through my pelvis and lumbar spine. I screamed, then collapsed back to the pavement, frustrated and afraid. The pain felt more horrendous than any I had ever experienced. I thought for a moment that my hips had been ripped from my body! At the very least, I thought that my back had been shattered.

In that moment I didn't fear death as much as I did the thought of never being able to walk again. I had enough consciousness left in my body to understand that the pain in my back and my inability to move were not good signs, and I had a very real chance coming out of this in a wheelchair.

Even then, with all of that pain and the gut-wrenching fear of paralysis running through my mind, my animal instinct still wanted my body to get up and flee as I continued to squirm in panic and desperation.

---

[3] My doctor later reported that this type of phenomenon was not unusual during traumatic events, at least in his experience. He had several patients who had experienced something similar.

Eventually, I managed to wiggle enough to get my head and shoulders to a point where they were out from under the front of the SUV.

I glanced over to my left and saw a pickup truck and a man with a cell phone. He seemed to be on the phone even as I whimpered something about calling for an ambulance. I turned my head to the right and saw the driver of the SUV. She screamed something to me in a foreign language. I had no idea what her words meant but my animal-mind didn't care — it wanted me to get up and confront her. I'm not terribly proud of that instinct now, but in hindsight I was in fight-or-flight mode. Since the pain was too intense to allow me to stand, I instead screamed back at her. With me yelling at her, she ran to the side of her vehicle and out of my line of sight. I later learned that she had jumped back into the driver's seat of the SUV and appeared to bystanders as if she were going to drive off.[4]

As I continued my struggle to get up and run, a blonde woman, a pony-tailed angel, ran up to me from my left. She knelt down next to me and said her name was Ann or Annie — I can't remember which now — and that she was a trauma nurse. She put her hands on my shoulders and gently told me not to move.

It turned out that this simple gesture saved me from becoming a paraplegic, and I am utterly grateful to her from the depths of my soul. Unknown to me at the time, my first lumbar vertebrae (L1) in my lower back had shattered. Any attempt to stand and that damaged vertebrae would have collapsed around my spinal cord, severing it and leaving me paralyzed.

Ann stayed with me until the first responders arrived, then she moved off to one side, still speaking with me to keep me calm.[5] In a rush, firemen, police, and paramedics converged on the scene. My body remained mostly under the SUV, so two paramedics knelt down next

---

[4] I later learned that concerned bystanders intervened and prevented her from any attempts to drive away. I'm very grateful to everyone who helped me at the scene that day — I owe them my life.

[5] Only one other person saw and interacted with Ann, one of the police officers, and the nurse said that she didn't want to give her name. The officer briefly spoke with her after my transfer to the hospital, then Ann disappeared into the crowd. The District Attorney's office attempted to locate her for several months, but all of their attempts failed. I still don't know who she is, but in that moment she was my guardian angel.

to me to try to figure out if I was pinned and how badly I was hurt. It turned out that my sternum was now free of the transfer case and the paramedics decided they could simply roll the truck backwards to free me. I heard the firemen yelling to the bystanders to clear the area. Several first responders then pushed the vehicle away so the paramedics could stabilize me for the trip to the nearest trauma center.

Once the truck was moved, the paramedics surrounded me. It was then that both parts of my consciousness finally came back together. I can't explain how it happened. One moment my mind was in two separate places and in the next, both parts were back together in my broken body. I didn't feel or experience anything different or unusual. I simply noticed that "I" was back to being in one place again.

The paramedics then did a check of my potential injuries. One of them gently cradled my neck in his hands. He gingerly touched my neck vertebrae one at a time and I screamed in pain. He then asked about other pain and I mumbled something about my lower back and pelvis.

Another of the paramedics managed to gently slide a hard, plastic collar around my neck, and eased my helmet and backpack off. With great care, three of them worked to slide me first onto a backboard, then a gurney. Ann stayed with me during all of this, asking me questions to keep me focused on her while the paramedics worked to stabilize me. She asked if I wanted her to go to the hospital with me. I said yes — I wanted company, someone friendly to hold my hand and help keep my panic at bay. But once the paramedics moved me into the ambulance, Ann disappeared. I never saw her again. She didn't accompany me to the hospital and I was never able to remember her full name. Whoever she was, I am truly grateful that she showed up that day just when I needed her.

The paramedics stabilized me in the ambulance as quickly and gently as possible. They locked the gurney to the floor with a loud click, then made sure the straps securing me to the backboard were snug. A medic asked me questions about my name, birth date, medical history, and allergies. My mind really wasn't focused on him, though, even as I answered his questions. Pain consumed me. It felt as though everything hurt — my neck, back, shoulders, thighs, and arms all complained. Nothing seemed *normal* anymore. And I just wanted everything to be normal again. I wanted to be running my errands. I wanted to enjoy my afternoon off, at home, working on an oil painting, cooking dinner, and watching a movie. But all of that would have to wait.

I did feel grateful for the short ride to the emergency room. In a way I was fortunate. The crash happened less than 1/2 mile from a hospital with a trauma center. The transport was a blur of IVs, vital signs, and EMTs making sure I was stable and not moving.

I don't remember arriving at the hospital or being wheeled out of the ambulance into the emergency room (ER), although what happened there remains clear in my mind.

Frenzied activity greeted me in the ER. The trauma nurses cut my clothes in order to check my injuries. While they performed their initial exam, I tried to deal with waves of pain ripping through my back and shoulder. I also remember whining about my clothes to the nurses — I had just purchased these cold-weather cycling clothes and they were goners on my first ride! Funny what your mind chooses to fixate on during a crisis.

While the trauma team continued their first round of evaluations — placing yet more IVs, taking vitals, looking for obvious bone breaks and scrapes on my skin — doctors tried to find a pain medicine I could tolerate. Like most members of my family, I'm particularly sensitive to most pain medications. Nonsteriodal anti-inflammatories (NSAIDs) were not an option since they can hinder bone healing and cause gastric bleeding. I also had a history of becoming violently ill with many other pain medications so I refused most everything the trauma team tried to give me. I could see frustration on their faces but being ill was the last thing I wanted in my current state.

While the doctors worked on managing my pain, nurses tried to contact my family on my partially-crushed phone. When I'd set out on my ride that morning, I'd placed my smartphone in its usual pocket on the outside of my backpack. During the crash the phone endured its own share of trauma as it was dragged on the ground, pinned in a pocket of my pack between me and the asphalt. Cracks now ran through its touchscreen but miraculously the phone itself still (barely) functioned. One of the doctors took a look at my phone and joked that it was a metaphor for my body: busted up but still working. I managed a chuckle and appreciated his lightening the mood.

One of the trauma nurses managed her way through the shattered screen of my phone and contacted my niece, Chrissy. Chrissy worked as a nurse at another hospital and, like me, was also sensitive to pain medications. She suggested an opioid pain medication that I might be able to tolerate, hydromorphone, and I agreed to try it.

Time slipped past in a blur of vitals and medical evaluations. It's odd to me now that I remained relatively calm through this time. I focused on managing my pain and contacting my friends and family. I didn't feel afraid — I simply wanted to know the full extent of my injuries, so I focused on being patient.

In the early afternoon, the imaging team came to transport me to another part of the hospital for more X-rays than I thought possible. After the first set of films, the radiologist decided that the X-rays didn't tell a clear enough story; another team then brought me to the CT scanner for a more thorough view of my injuries. After the CT scans, the imaging team rolled me back to the ER through one long corridor after another.

Next came more waiting while the radiologist and trauma team evaluated the CT scans.

By this point I had spent about four pain-filled hours in the ER and still no one had been able to give me a full rundown of my injuries. I knew I wasn't in good shape but at the same time I understood how fortunate I was to be conscious and still able to feel my legs. I wasn't allowed to move them, but I felt comforted by the fact that I could still *feel* them. But I was more scared about injuries that might be going unnoticed than I was about the obvious ones.

Everything that afternoon in the ER felt surreal, as if this was happening to someone else and couldn't possibly be me. My brain felt disconnected from the events around me, and it almost seemed as if I was simply a supporting cast member in some overly dramatic TV soap opera. Only it wasn't a TV show. It was my life, my body, my pain, and my future.

During the time I waited for the test and imaging results, I tried my best to have some phone conversations with my family. Unfortunately those attempted conversations were horribly muddled by my pain medication. For some reason, whether it was the injury to my head or the pain medications, I couldn't seem to form cohesive thoughts in my mind. My family and friends said that I sounded lucid, though, but I still don't remember any part of those conversations.

My niece lived in a different part of Denver and my sisters were thousands of miles away so I was still alone in the ER. This actually didn't bother me too much. At the time, I thought it would be easier to deal with any bad news if I was alone. It was terrible enough getting bad health news, but for me, receiving it in front of family or friends made coping more difficult. I always felt as though I needed to be strong for them and to make sure they were OK first, forgetting about myself or my own feelings in the process.

No, I was glad I was alone.

My family contacted my workplace and called a few of my local friends who would stop by a bit later.

My first visitors were the local police. Officers came in to speak to me at least twice between 2 and 3 PM. The first visit concerned the details of the accident itself. They took my statement, asked me questions about the crash and took photos of my injuries, my backpack, and my helmet. I remember only bits and pieces of this visit: seeing my shredded backpack, my cracked helmet, and hearing that my bike's frame was bent and twisted beyond repair. The officers left but came back about 45 minutes later to inform me about the driver and the consequences she would face. The officers indicated that since my injuries were quite severe, the driver would be charged for several different violations including driving without a license, driving without her prescription glasses, and failure to yield. The charges might change once the District Attorney's office reviewed the case but in any event, she would be spending some time in jail.

Quite frankly, I really didn't care one way or another what would happen to her. My mind was completely focused on my own injuries.

By 3 PM, a neurosurgeon arrived from Boulder. His expertise was in surgical intervention for severe back traumas and he came highly recommended by the hospital. As he approached my bed in the ER, the first thing I thought when looking at him was "Wow, he's too young to be a doctor." He looked to be around 25 years old, although I guessed his true age to be at least several years older than that. I didn't really care, though, as long as he could put Humpty Dumpty back together again.

My trauma doctor and one of the nurses arrived to consult with the surgeon. The surgeon studied my scans and proclaimed bluntly that it was a miracle I wasn't paralyzed or dead. I wasn't sure whether to be scared or relieved at that! The trauma team had previously told me that most people normally don't survive the type of accident I'd experienced, but it somehow felt even more ominous when the surgeon corroborated their sentiments.

All in all, I felt deeply grateful to have been spared.

After talking among themselves, the doctors came to my bedside to explain my injuries to me. Their expressions looked serious and solemn. A knot formed in the pit of my stomach. My fears chimed in and worried that my injuries were probably worse than I had thought.

The good news: I miraculously suffered very little bruising on my body which surprised everyone, including me. A small area on the front of my left shoulder held my only bruise. From its direct impact with the asphalt, I expected that the left side of my body would be black and blue for weeks. I felt relieved that wouldn't be the case. My own small sense of vanity didn't like the thought of massive amounts of bruising.

I was also grateful that I suffered very little road rash, just one small spot about the size of a quarter on my left shoulder. This surprised me even more than the lack of bruising! Anyone who's ever fallen from a bicycle can attest to how easy it is to have the road's surface shred your skin. And here I was, dragged along the pavement for 50 feet and no road rash to speak of. Wow, what a miracle! One of the nurses held up my backpack and showed me why my back wasn't shredded: my pack was. It had taken the brunt of the road's rough surface and saved my skin.

The neurosurgeon eventually chimed in and said all signs pointed to a full recovery in about a year to eighteen months.

I felt relieved at the "full recovery" part, but felt dread at the prospect of eighteen months of recovery. What in the world was wrong with me that would take eighteen months to heal?

I had a major concussion with bleeding apparent in my brain, a broken left collarbone, five broken ribs on my left side, bruised ribs on my right side, minor internal bleeding in my pelvic region, a minor crack in my pelvis, a cracked sternum, many compression fractures in my spine (neck, middle back, and lower back), my L1 (first lumbar) vertebrae shattered and burst apart in my lower back, and many transverse process[6] fractures up and down my spine.

In total, at least 24 of my bones were visibly broken, the majority of them in my spine. There may have been other, smaller fractures that were hidden with post-trauma swelling, too. The most immediate problem was my L1 vertebrae which had shattered and sent sharp bits of bone into my spinal canal, coming dangerously close to severing my spinal cord. I was within a millimeter or so of being a paraplegic. That made me sit up and take notice, so to speak.

Another shocking thing was that my neck injuries were so severe that I was close to being paralyzed from any one of them, too. My neck hurt less than my back but the fractures and ligament damage there were so traumatic that any ill-timed movement could cause the damaged

---

6 Transverse processes are the spurs of bone that jut out from the sides of the spinal column.

vertebrae to shift out of place and sever my spinal cord. I was hovering close to being a quadriplegic. That sobered me more than anything else. The thought of my legs not working was hard enough — I could likely deal with that in time — but the possibility of having my entire body paralyzed was more than I could conceive of.

I went into a form of shock at that point. My mind didn't want to deal with any of the bad news: the broken bones, the potential for paralysis, or the brain injury. In fact, a part of me wanted to pretend that everything was A-OK. I tried to convince myself that I wasn't very badly injured and would be back to my normal activities in record time.

Unfortunately, things didn't quite turn out the way I thought they would.

The trauma team installed a hard, more permanent, plastic brace around my neck that they said would be my constant companion for the next three months. "Great," I thought. But at least with this on, my neck would heal completely given enough time, and I wouldn't need surgery.

My most damaged vertebrae, the first lumbar in my lower back, would need stabilization as soon as possible, though. To do that, the surgeon recommended installing titanium rods from the T12 vertebrae (12th thoracic, just below my ribcage) to L2 (2nd lumbar, toward my pelvis) to take the pressure off the burst vertebrae, allowing it to heal. The titanium rods would stabilize my spine and, in time, those three vertebrae would fuse together and effectively become one large bone.

While the surgery might sound traumatic, I was in favor of it and didn't hesitate in giving the surgeon my consent. The only non-surgical alternative was three or more months flat on my back in a body cast, hoping that everything would heal correctly. Having the rods in place would allow me to have my mobility while my body healed.

Give me the titanium, please!

It was now early evening and I still lay flat on my back in the ER. The hospital admissions staff scheduled surgery for the following Monday morning — three days away. Finally, around 6 PM, nurses moved me from the ER to my very own private room in the intensive care unit (ICU).

Friends and coworkers came in to visit me that evening. I don't remember much about their time with me. The opioids and letdown from the trauma made me feel sleepy and unfocused. I do remember that their compassion and kindness touched me deeply and made me feel supported and cared for. I also began to see that many people were rooting for me to recover, and I wasn't as alone as I thought I was. I felt a sense of love and happiness inside of me, even through all of my physical pain.

I spent that Saturday and Sunday flat on my back in my ICU room, using the opioid to keep the pain under control. So much of my body cried out in pain: my broken ribs, my collarbone, my sternum, my neck, my pelvis, and my back. Even with the medication, my pain wasn't under "control." I still felt the sensations of pain but the medication put my mind in a state where I really didn't care about the pain, or anything else for that matter. I wasn't allowed to get up, but then again I didn't want to. Even with the medication, the pain was horrendous and I still battled fears for my future. I did everything I could to stay calm and in control of my emotions, including meditation and distracting myself with visitors or TV, but sometimes I slipped into panic and worry. Friends and family graciously helped me regain hope and sat with me through those terrifying moments when I feared my very active life was over. My niece, her fiancé, and her daughter, came to help me stay calm, take care of my home, and keep my mind occupied. Friends and coworkers visited to check up on me and try to lift my spirits with care packages of books, magazines, toiletries, and art supplies. Their visits warmed my heart and soul, even if I couldn't concentrate for long enough to put their gifts to good use.

Having my family and friends visit me helped — their love and support kept my mind on the goal: surgery on Monday, then healing.

CHAPTER 2

Surgery

MOST PEOPLE DON'T LOOK FORWARD to Mondays.

I usually counted myself in that group, but today was my first step in getting my mobility back, so my impatience could not be held in check.

The hours before the surgery stretched on for what seemed like forever. I am grateful for the presence of two women who stayed with me during this time: Ellen, the aunt of a former partner, and Angela, my friend and manager at my workplace. Their loving presence kept me calmer and focused on something besides my impatience and fear in those hours before surgery.

While I just wanted the surgery over with, at the same time I dreaded it. The thought of being anesthetized and having my back reconstructed frightened me even though I knew it was my best option for achieving a full recovery.

I never have liked going under the knife. Three prior surgeries years before left me a little skittish about the anesthesia. I hated the forced loss of consciousness and, like many people, always had that nagging fear of not waking up. On top of that, some of the anesthesia drugs made me nauseated and ill upon waking. I have a medical history of reacting to both pain medication and anesthesia and I was about to need whopping doses of both, which worried me. And I was not looking forward to the long, possibly painful, recovery this time.

I tried to distract myself in conversation with Angela and Ellen but that didn't work very well. My mind kept running off to wallow in fear, not leaving me much mental energy for my visitors. My mind fixated on the thought that the surgery would somehow go terribly wrong.

Paradoxically, a part of me also wanted this to just be the end of it all. I'm not proud now of thinking this way, but constant, throbbing pain wracked my body even with the hydromorphone. The pain was so intense that I didn't want to go on living if it was always going to be like this. And that morning, I assumed the pain would always be this bad. I just couldn't seem get my mind wrapped around the concept of a pain-free future, and didn't have much hope that the procedure would bring me back to normal even though my surgeon assured me otherwise. My back continued to feel like it was being ripped in half even though I was doped up on hefty painkillers, and horror stories of spinal fusions not working played through my mind in a continuous loop. Sometimes too much knowledge isn't a good thing.

Something even more subtle scared me more though: going back home to the same life I had before — a life that was unfulfilling. While I hadn't been *unhappy* before my crash, I wasn't all that happy either. It felt as though I was simply going through the motions of life, stuck in a predictable rut, not very excited about any one thing, and not knowing what to do to make a change. My writing job was stable but I was having trouble getting my real passion, my art career, to take off. I enjoyed painting for its own sake but I also wanted to sell my works and teach art and creativity. Painting was (and is) very enjoyable for me, but I also wanted it to generate income. The fact that it wasn't doing that yet disheartened me.

Even worse was my daily life before the crash. I felt lonely. It was this feeling of being utterly alone that bothered me the most. I remember thinking that close family members would miss me if for some reason I didn't make it through surgery, and some friends, but I didn't have much more than that, at least in my own mind.

I finally faced my own truth: in the last couple of years I had somehow managed to isolate myself in my own little corner of the world. *I did this to myself.* While isolation felt emotionally safer at some level, in that hospital bed waiting for surgery I came to realize its terrible price on my soul. I wasn't active in getting out and enjoying the community, I didn't attend arts events anymore, and certainly didn't socialize with friends as I used to. My connection to those around me felt tenuous at best and I knew something about this isolated life was not *me*.

I knew then that, no matter what, my life needed to change.

Ellen, Angela, and I waited for the surgery longer than we thought was necessary, until finally it became obvious that something was delayed. Nurses came in to my room periodically to check on me, then around 2 PM the anesthesiologist arrived to brief me on his role. It was to be routine from his perspective. He already knew which set of drugs he'd use — ones that had been used on me in past surgeries, plus a couple more to keep nausea at bay. In his view, everything was predictable.

That sounded promising.

Closer to 3 PM, my surgeon and his team arrived to explain the actual procedure in more detail. After I was in the operating room (OR) and anesthetized, they would move me, face-down, on to the operating table. The surgeon would open an incision along my lower back, pull the muscles and other tissues out of the way, and clean out the dangerous bits of vertebrae near my spinal cord. Next, they would attach titanium rods across my three lower-back vertebrae to stabilize the one that had burst. Eventually, all three vertebrae would fuse together into one piece of solid, safe bone.

Piece of cake.

The surgery itself would last about two hours, after which I'd be brought back into recovery and eventually return to ICU. The surgeon reiterated that he expected me to achieve a full recovery after the vertebrae healed together. Good news for me, although a part of me didn't fully believe him. But even with the fear of the procedure failing in some way I still tried to hope for the best. I didn't want to give up my active lifestyle and while I was OK with making some modifications to my activities, I didn't want to become a couch potato for the rest of my life.

I trusted my doctor, but the surgery sounded horribly complicated and physically brutal. I just wanted to feel human again. I wanted to be whole, active, and pain-free.

The surgeon went on to say that the afternoon's prior procedure had run late so the start of mine would be delayed a bit more. I wasn't happy about the delay but was powerless to do anything about it, either. Fear combined with painkillers left me emotionally fragile and very worried, but I did my best to put the fears aside. That worked — mostly.

At 4 PM, an hour later than the originally scheduled start time, one of the nurses came to wheel me to the operating room. Finally! While I still felt fear, I just wanted the surgery over. I said a quiet goodbye to Angela and Ellen, then spent the next few minutes trying to stay calm as the nurse wheeled me through the corridors.

"Deep breaths," I thought.

I called on years of meditation practice in a attempt to calm myself. It didn't work. My throat tightened with fear, my mouth felt like cotton was stuffed inside it, and swallowing was almost impossible.

CHAPTER 3

Another World

THE DOORS OF THE OPERATING room stood in front of me, gleaming white from the bright surgical lights shining through their windows. An odd thought about the doors' resemblance to the Pearly Gates passed through my mind, but I tried to put that aside. I didn't want to somehow jinx myself or the surgical team. The pit of my stomach tightened again and I felt yet another wave of panic wash through my body.

More deep breaths.

As the nurse pushed me inside, I noticed the unusual color of the room: bright, sunflower yellow instead of the usual cold, sterile white I'd come to expect in hospitals. Metal equipment that seemed impossibly shiny ranged around the room, and the surgical team stood on the opposite side of the operating table. I spied a tray with what I assumed were surgical instruments laid out around it and a bit of terror grabbed at my stomach again. I wished I hadn't seen them.

I didn't pay much attention to the nurse as she prepped my IV tubing and anesthesia drugs, and I hardly noticed the anesthesiologist come up on my left side. Instead, I devoted most of my mental energy to stilling my nervousness. The anesthesiologist adjusted the IV drip and joked about it being time for cocktails, then I drifted off.

I've had three previous surgeries that required the same general anesthesia as I was getting today — two abdominal and one minor back procedure. I've also endured a few minor surgeries requiring the same or similar anesthesia. None of those experiences were remarkable in any way. In all of them, the anesthesiologist gave me the drugs, I drifted off into a gray state of nothingness[7] (I wouldn't call it "sleep"), and what felt like the next second I was waking up in the recovery room. No memories, no dreams, no sense of anything happening, just the experience of slipping into a gray unconsciousness one second and waking up in recovery the next.

Not this time.[8]

I did drift off as the anesthesiologist gave me my "cocktail," but it wasn't to the gray state of nothingness that I expected.[9]

I abruptly found myself standing in a spectacular landscape unlike any I'd ever experienced. Warm breezes drifted across my skin. Beautiful vistas of meadows and distant mountains surrounded me. And a pervasive, loving presence overwhelmed me in its intensity.

My mind tried to wrap itself around what was happening since it felt so real. In the back of my awareness I knew I had just gone into surgery, but I wondered if I had somehow dreamed the bike accident and my injuries. This place felt more real to me than any on Earth.

Surrounding me was a landscape of gently rolling hills, flower-filled grassy meadows, towering deciduous trees in full leaf, trees taller and more grand than any here on Earth, and a sense of a light mist floating through as if it were a humid summer morning. The sky gleamed a very light, pearly blue, similar to what you might see at the ocean's shore, with wispy clouds and a very bright but somewhat diffuse light.

---

7 If you haven't been in surgery, having anesthesia may seem odd and unfamiliar. It's not sleep. It's really a state of unconsciousness. It's characterized by lack of memory, lack of pain, and muscle relaxation (wikipedia.org). You don't dream.

8 What happened? Due to a reaction to the anesthesia, my blood pressure and heart rate plummeted to almost zero for a short time. According to my medical team, this is enough to trigger a true NDE.

9 From here on, things get difficult to explain in human words. Much of what I experienced in Heaven was pure knowing and feeling. While I do my best to describe them to you, know that mere words cannot even begin to adequately explain what I experienced there.

Oddly, though, I didn't see or hear any evidence of other people or animal life. No one else walked the meadows. No fences, roads, or buildings intruded on the landscape. No birds sung from the branches or flew through the air. It was just me, this gorgeous landscape, and that loving presence permeating it all.

I had the sense that I was standing. I could tell I wasn't floating since the ground felt solid under my bare feet as I walked. Lightweight clothes fit for a summer day seemed to drape softly over my skin. They felt silky, but I didn't have the sense to look down to check them out. I guess I'm not much of a fashionista.

My surroundings captured most of my attention. Below the surface forms and colors of everything in the landscape, I somehow also saw or sensed vibrating energy. I'm not sure how to describe it. It seemed I could see the surface of a leaf, for example, yet also see below it to an energy, a vibration of love or compassion or kindness that made the leaf take on a subsurface radiance. Everything had this radiance: trees, grass, sky, flowers, and clouds. Colors seemed intensified by this radiance. The feeling of love flowed through everything and heightened this radiance.

Through it all I sensed and somehow physically felt an incredibly profound feeling of peace, rightness, goodness, and love flowing through my body. I cried, literally wept, at how beautiful it all was and thought to myself that it was definitely an OK place to be during my surgery; much better than that gray nothingness I expected. I didn't know *where* I stood or how I came here, but I felt at home, right, and at peace.

The Beauty I saw and felt in those first moments really does deserve a capital "B." It wasn't just pleasing to the eye, there was something deeper to it, more harmonious, more blessed, and more powerful. Everything felt tied together by an enormous amount of love and peace. Somehow I knew that the beauty of the landscape around me was the product of unconditional love on a cosmic scale.

While this beauty took my breath away, the sense of overwhelming peace and love completely ensnared me and made me want to stay here forever. I continued to feel a deep sense of unconditional love flow through all things around me: the air, the ground below my feet, the trees, the clouds, and me. I didn't know how it was possible to feel love as if it were a physical presence, but I did. My *being* vibrated with love to its core. Every molecule of me seemed bathed in love. I couldn't block it out, nor would I have wanted to. I continued to feel the energy of love flow around me like a gentle current, washing through me, and eventually capturing me by the heart. I felt supported by some kind of loving presence so powerful, yet so gentle, that I cried again. I had never experienced such unconditional love and acceptance in all of my years on this Earth.

It felt as though this place were built from love on a very grand, cosmic scale.

Soon, a visitor joined me. As she approached, she welcomed me with a warm embrace of pure love.

CHAPTER 4

My Guide

EVEN AFTER JUST A FEW moments, I knew that I didn't want to leave. By then I started to wonder if I had died on the operating table and was on my way to whatever existence came next. I remembered hearing vague stories of people dying in surgery and having experiences they attributed to an afterlife, so I began to wonder if this was happening to me, too.

It wasn't until a figure in a human-like shape appeared to me that I realized something was very different than my previous surgeries. This figure approached silently from slightly behind me and to my right, coming in to view as if she emerged from mists. Her hazy, gradual fading-into-being seemed somehow natural for this place.

She greeted me with an energy-embrace of pure love. Love emanated from her and surrounded me. She didn't touch me with her hands or enfold me into a hug, she simply sent me waves of loving energy as a welcome.

She wasn't recognizable as someone I'd known from life. I wondered if she was a spiritual being of some kind sent to bring me to whatever comes next. I hoped that was the case — I had already fallen in love with this place and wanted her to help me stay here.

While she appeared to be human, I sensed and saw that "human" wasn't really the correct term for her. Her general appearance was female but I got the feeling that the form she held was one she took solely for me. The form seemed somehow *convenient* for now, and later she confirmed this for me. I did get a sense of a deeply feminine presence, though.

She appeared to stand a few inches taller than me with a slim figure and long, brown, wavy hair that fell almost to her waist. Her face was a little indistinct. It was as if I couldn't catch a really good glimpse of it or it was slightly blurred. I felt frustrated — I wanted to *really* see her. What I could see of her face was pleasant enough but not remarkable in any way. She was not terribly beautiful but not unpleasant to my eyes, either. She wore a loose, luminescent, light pearl-gray, long-sleeved, tunic-type of shirt that draped and flowed beautifully over and around her. The fabric also glowed with a pearlescent sparkle of energy that radiated into the air around her body. This radiant energy was similar to what I had already sensed under the surface of everything in the landscape. She also wore either a long skirt or full, drapey pants of the same fabric as the shirt — I couldn't really decide which. The fabric of her clothing looked as if it might be a nicely worn-in linen, or linen mixed with silk.

Kindness, compassion, and caring radiated from her face and I felt that she held that deep love for me in a way I had never experienced before from anyone. Not romantic love, but a love you might expect from an angel or a saint or the Creator. I also felt a profound, expansive love coming through her as if she was a transmitter, radiating out from her and enfolding me in its warm embrace as if she too were made of it. Somehow, she was able to embrace me with loving energy without even touching me. The love coming from her made me relax into her presence as if she were a sister or trusted friend.

In hindsight, being able to feel love and energy flowing through me seems strange. After all, it's not how we humans normally experience things in our own lives. We touch with our skin, hear things with our ears, and see with our eyes. But the only things we typically feel are our own internal emotions, or things such as body pain, discomfort, or other physical sensations. We feel heat or a chill through our skin, but as humans we don't typically feel love as a physical force.

But in that place, love felt like a normal, physical force.

She never did tell me her name or *what* she was. I didn't even think to question this while I was there, but it seems strange that I didn't ask. For now I'll simply refer to her as "my Guide" to keep things simple. I felt that she was a being of love, perhaps even a spiritual being. But I can't put her into a category familiar to me. For now it's enough to think of her as simply a spiritual being who had some interest in helping me. The only thing that mattered to me was that she acted as my mentor and guide during my stay in that place.

My Guide strolled with me. We marveled at the flowers that vibrated with colors I can't describe. The trees formed a canopy overhead, pearly light filtered through the leaves, the blue sky beyond, and that sense of utter peace and love suffused everything. I enjoyed walking, feeling healthy again with no pain, sensing the cool grass beneath my bare feet and the warm breezes on my face.

My Guide seemed to flow over the ground. I didn't see that she took steps or made physical contact with the landscape. She just flowed gracefully, accompanying me through this beautiful place. At times I fell to my knees and sat there in utter amazement and gratitude at the beauty and love around me.

We continued to move among the meadows and into more glades of trees. I sensed that the landscape fell away or disappeared behind me as we meandered along. I questioned that in my mind, and my Guide answered it without me even uttering a word. She somehow *knew* what I was thinking! And yes, in some strange way, the landscape behind me did fall away as we continued our tour.

In time, as I grew more comfortable in her presence, my Guide began telling me more about this place. I wasn't in Heaven *per se*, just in a place to prepare me for what was to come — a slice of Heaven you might call it. There isn't a good word to describe it in our language, though. A human equivalent would be if you could equate Heaven to a cathedral, I was in the vestibule as you come in the exterior doors, but before you enter the main doors into the nave (the main worship area).

I was in the waiting area. Heaven's green room.[10]

A glimmer of hope that I'd soon see the *real* Heaven sparked in my heart. If this was the waiting area, just imagine how amazing the full experience of Heaven would be!

She went on to explain that she chose to be a voice to me from many others *beyond* where we were now. I got the impression that these were spiritual beings or souls who somehow communicated to me through her. She was a representative of sorts, a speaker, one who came here to teach me and to help me start on the next part of my journey. I thought she meant I was going to die and the next part of my journey was to go on to the afterlife. Frankly, I hoped that was the case. If what awaited was anything like this place I would gladly follow her there.

I didn't *know* what was beyond. I couldn't see it in any way, although I had a sense of *others* out there who I could not see. I also got the impression from my Guide that more existed than what I was experiencing. I was OK not knowing, and still am. I'm comfortable with many aspects of my experience remaining part of a greater mystery.

It turns out I was very wrong about what my future held. What came next was something I wouldn't have expected — not in a million years.

She began communicating information to me, messages or lessons that those in Heaven wanted to pass along to me and to others back on Earth. These teachings or messages were concepts that Spirit suffused them with constantly; knowledge that was an innate part of *this place* as it was *beyond* here. These messages contained knowledge that many of us on Earth seem to have either forgotten or never learned but were an integral part of existence in Heaven.

These messages somehow helped to form or strengthen the structure there. Every spiritual entity somehow participated in these teachings, and much more knowledge as well. This part was fuzzy to me — I

---

10 Even though I actually visited a "pre-heaven," for clarity's sake, I will use the term "Heaven" through the rest of the book.

still struggle with describing this collective knowledge and how the spiritual world interacted with it.

My Guide communicated to me that the messages were initially intended for me so that I could improve my own life. I was being given the opportunity to make my own life one that I truly wanted to live. What a gift!

The messages were also meant to be shared with others to reinforce what we might learn in our faith or spirituality. In some instances, they might be the start of someone coming to learn about spiritual matters — the introduction to deeper knowledge and mysteries.

She explained that in the past, I volunteered to serve by being a messenger of these teachings. At some time, perhaps before I was born into my life, I had apparently made an agreement to serve light and love in whatever way Spirit thought best. My Guide actually placed a vision in my mind of this happening. I stood with others in a light-filled room and agreed to be a kind of messenger. I couldn't really see the details of those others, though, I simply sensed their presence and heard their words.

But I still had a hard time believing that I somehow made an agreement *before I was born*. How could that happen? What if I changed my mind didn't want to do it?

My Guide explained that souls often agree to different kinds of tasks before they are born into life. We might refer to these as *callings*. Some tasks are small in scope, and some, like Nelson Mandela's, are large, but they're all voluntary. I volunteered for my little task of being a messenger of these insights to as many people as needed to hear them.

My waking self on Earth had no conscious memory of this agreement, but my Guide gently reminded me of it. She made it clear that now was the time where I'd be fulfilling my part of the contract. But since it was voluntary, I could also decide not to follow this calling. I wouldn't face anger or retribution if I walked away from the task.

A very palpable sense of the weight of responsibility overwhelmed me. I almost physically felt a weight settle on my shoulders and I questioned whether I was up to the task. But it seems I had no choice in my own soul. I *wanted* to do this at a very deep level, and felt compelled in some way to take on this task.

My lessons with this spiritual being kicked off.

We strolled again through the landscape, communicating many things that the spiritual beings in that *beyond* wanted us here on Earth to understand. I felt a little like Luke Skywalker being schooled by The Force through Yoda.

The landscape continued to amaze me. Colors vibrated in harmony with different emotions. Trees weren't necessarily green nor was the sky always blue. They hummed with an inner energy and colors that radiated love, gratitude, and joy. Sometimes the trees would open up and I saw distant, low mountains shimmering on the horizon. Mists shrouded their flanks, and like everything else, they too seemed to radiate a deep, internal energy.

I thought it was odd that I didn't hear anything except a soft whisper of breezes through the tree leaves, and the voice of my guide when she needed to speak to me.

I know this might all sound bizarre, as if I was on some LSD trip gone wrong, but it made sense to me then and still does now. My Guide explained that what I saw as landscape was, in part, created by my own interaction with this place. Spirit wanted me to feel safe and comfortable here, so I was surrounded by a landscape that would seem familiar to me. Somehow my individual thoughts and feelings helped to shape the things I saw and how I experienced them. I saw rolling hills and beautiful trees interspersed with grassy, flower-filled meadows. But another visitor might be in a valley with towering mountains all around, or perhaps sitting on a warm beach somewhere in the tropics. It seemed as though this place was, in part, a participatory experience.

That's also why my Guide appeared in her form, as a human woman. That form was comfortable for me, friendly and nurturing. What I saw in her and in the landscape was, in part, crafted specifically for me. But the underpinnings that I sensed, the love, the presence, and the radiant energy, formed the structure of *all* of Heaven. That was the core upon which all else was built.

Wow. I had a hard time coming to grips with that concept. As I tried to let that sink in, we continued to meander among the trees.

Sometimes she talked, passing on information like you and I might as colleagues at work. Other times the communication was more spiritually-based. These spiritual communications came to me as feelings and impressions straight into my mind and heart. Sometimes I simply felt a sense of immediate knowing, other times I experienced feelings and visuals mixed with words. This non-verbal method of communicating seemed strange at first but it didn't take long before it became natural.

As she continued to teach me, I realized that the spiritual realm operated very differently from Earth. Verbal communication is not at all preferred in Heaven. In fact, it seemed a rather awkward and unclear form of sending and receiving knowledge. Somehow in that place, in that spiritual realm of which I had only a small glimpse, the beings there use many more profound forms of communication. These other forms are more direct, beautiful, and loving than anything we experience here on Earth.

Information still flooded into my being. I struggled to remember it all but she said not to worry. Everything was there, locked in my mind.

The messages she passed on to me encompassed the basics — Spirit 101 is my term for it. She, and those who spoke through her, communicated to me the nature of love, community, gratitude, companionship, how we're all connected spiritually, that we're never alone, and so much more. I'll cover these messages fully in Part II of this book.

At times during the communication I somehow felt collective emotions from those other spiritual beings — from soaring joy to terrible sadness — for certain events, ideas, and feelings in our society. I couldn't see these beings or souls, I just "heard" and felt many layers of knowledge and feeling coming in to me. At these times, the emotions came through as emotionally-charged "waves" in my body. Imagine a wind of electricity that instead of brushing over your skin and continuing on, literally goes right through every cell of you.

The other spiritual beings that my Guide represented were able to communicate their emotions and thoughts to me through her. I'm still not sure how this works or how to describe it. I just sensed that, at times, the knowledge and emotions of *many beings* were coming to me.

Several times the intensity of those collective thoughts and feelings was too great. My mind was still tied to my humanity and just could not deal with cosmic-sized thoughts and feelings. My knees buckled and I fell onto the ground as I struggled to process everything that came in. Those spiritual beings felt soaring joy when, through us, they witnessed our births or deaths. They see a human death in joyful terms; to them, that soul is finally and fully coming home. Sadness comes when they see how many of us hate ourselves, treat ourselves or our loved ones poorly, feel that we are separate from Spirit and each other, or convince ourselves that we're somehow not worthy or special enough to experience happiness and joy.

After I recovered from feeling those spiritual emotions, my Guide explained my part: it would be my task to put the messages into a form that I and other humans could understand. My job was to synthesize what she communicated to me, give it a human perspective, and then disseminate the information to as many people as possible, starting with me and my family. She again assured me that the knowledge was planted deep inside of me now.

I felt terrified to the core of my being and began to panic. A wave of fear rolled through my core.

Even though I knew that I *would* do this, *had* to do it, was bound spiritually to do it, the thought of being some kind of a messenger scared me silly. Who would believe me? Would I be mocked or called a fool?

I feared my friends and family would think I was nuts. I knew I would lose credibility among some of my scientist friends, and I realized that some people I'd known for years might choose to end their friendships with me. I feared the ridicule, the disbelief, and the character attacks because I certainly hadn't lived a saintly life. Lastly, I feared how profoundly my life might change.

And worst of all, *why* would anyone believe me?

I'm a relative *nobody*. I'm not much different from anyone else — a fairly normal scientist, artist, and writer. I'm not a spiritual guru, a saint, a priest, or a nun. I haven't given up my life in service to a religion. I've made mistakes — a lot of them. And to top it off, I don't believe in all of this anyway. Why would anyone give what I had to say a second thought?

But I knew deep in my heart that my old life was about to die and something new would take its place. The new life would somehow be based on this experience, although not fully defined by it. But I felt fear because I didn't know what my future would look or feel like in detail. Even though my life hadn't really been working well and I thought I wanted something new, at first I feared the new life because it was unknown. I feared surrendering to the task and to Spirit.

I also knew that I didn't have a choice. In the core of my being, I realized and *felt* that I had made a very deep commitment to serve and didn't want to renege on that commitment. Who was I to turn down God?

I began an internal struggle about this assignment that felt as though it lasted hours or even days. Maybe it did in Heaven's time.

I could sense my Guide getting a little weary of my doubt and struggles. Perhaps to her, assignments like this are normal but for me this seemed a much bigger task than I would ever want or could ever accomplish.

Suddenly, she surprised me by laying down in the middle of one of the meadows we'd wandered into, inviting me to join her like little children would, laying in the tall grasses and staring up at the sky. She seemed to be trying to help ease my fears a little by interjecting some lightness and play. It worked. We stared up into the shimmering cobalt blue sky, watching the clouds drift by and giggling like little girls. We were simply friends out enjoying the warm, sunny, summer day and gazing up into the sky looking for rabbits and dragons and horses camouflaged as clouds. I had some moments of fun staring up into that beautiful, shimmering blueness, trying to name shapes that came and went as quickly as a breath.

Spotting cloud animals in Heaven — what a trip! I assumed that a spiritual existence would be all seriousness, solemnity, and stern faces but she allowed me to see how playful, loving, and joy-filled it could be.

As we watched the clouds and picked out animal shapes, I had a sudden insight that this spiritual being next to me had been a friend for a very long time[11]. I still can't place her from this life I have now, but it seemed we were long-lost friends catching up after many years apart.

She stayed there with me, remaining quiet and letting everything sink in to my mind while I watched the sky. I completely enjoyed the peace and love of this place and still felt amazed at the sense of a loving Presence permeating everything. I didn't want to give any of that up. I couldn't imagine leaving even though I had been told that I would return to Earth.

In hindsight, I think she was giving me one last chance to enjoy that place before coming back to life on Earth, and to a broken body lying in a hospital.

Eventually she rolled over onto her side and looked at me saying, "I need to go soon, and it's time for you to get back to your life." She rose to her feet and held out her hand to help me up.

Panic and anger flared through me. I did NOT want to go back. I suspected that what awaited me there would be difficult, painful, and

---

[11] It's difficult to describe how time operated in Heaven. I definitely experienced time differently from its passage here on Earth. On Earth, you might say that at most I spent two hours in Heaven because the surgery lasted two hours. But when I was there, it felt like a lifetime, and no time, all at once. Yes, it's a paradox, one that I might never be able to understand or explain.

emotionally wrenching. Recovering from a terribly traumatic crash had enormous challenges but I knew that with this project I'd taken on, my life would profoundly change. That change terrified me.

Grudgingly, I allowed her to help me stand. I grasped her hand and she pulled me up. I was a mess: sobbing, protesting that I didn't want to go back to my life, that I wanted to go with her on to the real Heaven. Even though I had a commitment to keep, a part of me desperately wanted to stay. This was not a proud moment for me. I became like a toddler throwing a temper tantrum! I felt terrified to go back to my broken body, and to the unknown of the weeks and months ahead.

I believe that my Guide wanted me to have full knowledge, to prepare me for the way ahead, so she gave me a glimpse of my immediate future. It wasn't easy to watch and, in a way, confirmed some of my fears. She showed me the painful breakup of a relationship, being alone for a long stretch of time, and that the road ahead for me would be hard, not just physically, but emotionally, too. I didn't want to face it and didn't want to return.

My Guide sensed my fears and assured me that in the long term I would be financially OK, I would be looked after by Spirit, and would be very happy. She allowed me a glimpse of that future life of happiness with a loving partner, and a sense of deep fulfillment, but that time felt a long way off to me.

Even with the possibility that the mission I'd accepted could change my life for the better, I still wanted to go on with her. If this place was simply the portal to Heaven, Heaven itself must be amazing, I thought.

Who would have guessed I'd be arguing with a spiritual being shortly after she gave me a mission to complete?

But the truth was that I really didn't want to leave. Who would? When I was there I felt the love of a spiritual presence through every atom of my being. That love was a warmth from inside, supportive and light. I felt embraced, accepted, understood, part of an amazing family of beings of love and light, and a very real, tangible part of Creation. I didn't want to leave it, not for a second.

She stayed firm in her stance and insisted that I had accepted a mission, that I had agreed to go back to Earth and serve others by passing along these teachings. And she once again insisted that it was time for her to leave.

Even though I knew it was a losing battle, I resisted. I didn't want to go back. I wanted to accompany her. But what I wanted in that moment didn't make any difference.

She still insisted on sending me back.

But before she sent me home, she explained that she would help me a little, to make things a bit easier for me when I returned to my body. We were now standing, facing each other. She gently raised her right arm and placed that hand on my left shoulder, at the exact spot where my collarbone was broken. I didn't feel much contact from her hand, just a brief touch and warm energy, then she moved on to my left ribs. She placed her hand on my left side for a moment, then went on to my upper chest just below my throat. She briefly touched her fingertips on my upper sternum, then pulled her hand back.

I could feel her sadness as she looked at me. "It really is time for me to leave now. And it is time for you to go back to where you belong."

As she turned away from me to leave, another wave of dread, fear, and anger washed through me. I opened my mouth to argue again but I suddenly awoke in a bed, confused and sobbing. Through blurred vision, I saw people milling about the room but none of them were the woman with whom I had just spent what felt like weeks. I already missed her more than I can express. Her loss and the loss of that place caused waves of grief to course through my entire body.

I wanted her at my side to ease my fears and I couldn't understand why she wasn't with me anymore. Tears flowed down my cheeks. I felt as a child would, pulled away from its mother by strangers, knowing it would be a very long time before I'd see her again. The struggle to come to grips with being on Earth again, began.[12]

---

[12] For the next year or more, I would go through short periods of grief over the loss I felt from having to leave Heaven.

My senses returned slowly to the here and now of the recovery room. I remembered that I had been through surgery but I still felt confused as to where I had *been* and who my Guide was. And the tears of loss still ran down my cheeks. I'm sure the nurses wondered what was going on, why I cried, but I ignored them, mired in my grief at the loss of that glorious place.

In time I began to pay more attention to the recovery room. Doctors and nurses moved about, and my friend Angela appeared at my side. My surgeon eventually stopped in to check on me — I remember telling him in what seemed like a far-off voice that my back already felt better. He again reiterated that in his opinion I would recover fully in time.

I thought he might be right in saying that I would physically recover just fine, but I wondered if mentally, emotionally, or spiritually I'd ever be the same.

Part Two

Messages from Spirit

CHAPTER 5

The Messages

—◦≫≪◦—

You've reached the heart of the book. It's OK if you skipped ahead to this chapter to get right into the best part. Use this book in whatever way works best in your life.

What Exactly are the "Messages"?

The *messages, lessons,* or *insights* are just some of the ideas that my Guide wanted to pass on to us so that we could live better lives. These messages are the main concepts given to me during my time with her. She initially directed these insights to me specifically to help me improve my own life, and she thought others might benefit as well.

Before I was returned to my life, my Guide asked me to share what I learned from these messages with as many people as possible. Well, it wasn't so much of an *asking* as it was reminding me of what I had already agreed to do. The delivery formats would be left up to me, although the picture she placed in my mind was that of a book.

For many months, though, I dragged my feet on writing it. Even knowing who asked me to take on the work, and understanding the benefit it could have for many people, I procrastinated. My ego got in the way. I still harbored fears that I'd be looked upon as some kind of oddball, a crazy woman, or a liar. That all I wanted was attention or notoriety, or I was simply capitalizing on a tragic event. My fears of what others might think kept me from starting this project for months.

In the spring of 2014, I tentatively began documenting my experience in my blog (TheSpiritWay.Blogspot.com). I thought this forum might satisfy my Guide so that I could let the book project fade into nothingness.

Something strange happened while writing my blog. The writing process forced me to think through and meditate deeply on the information. People who read my blog also gave me feedback about how the messages impacted them. Their experiences with these insights encouraged me to continue writing. My blog became my way of processing both the near-death experience itself and the knowledge I'd come away with. I internalized what I learned and ended up working through my fears of what others might think. The beauty and power of my Guide's gift of wisdom settled into my being, and I no longer feared for my reputation. I understood that this information isn't for everyone, but that's OK. Shoving my ego aside, I realized it was time for the information to speak for itself.

These insights are not the complete set of knowledge bouncing around in Heaven, nor are they meant to replace our faith, religion, or belief systems. They're our birthright, though, information that we carry with us deep in our souls that we often forget when we become enmeshed in the drama of everyday life. These messages are meant to provide some practical help and ideas for living a great life, geared toward where we humans exist now in this time and place.

My understanding of the messages is this: these are some of the spiritual concepts we remember when we finally leave our human existence and return to that realm. These messages are a part of that spiritual reality. They are common knowledge, part of the expression of love that Spirit has for each and every one of us. It's difficult to explain in human terms because to us it makes little sense when I say that these truths, and others, help shape the structure or fabric of that existence. They are a part of the reality of that place just like gravity is a part of the reality of life on this Earth. Gravity influences everything here, we can't get away from it, and it forms part of the structure of our physical existence. In a similar way, these truths are part of the reality in the spiritual realm. Since the energy of that place is here on Earth too, in us and through everything, these teachings belong here as well. We know these messages at the level of our souls but they often get lost inside the living of our everyday human lives.

Learning to incorporate these messages now can greatly improve how we live and experience life. These insights can help bring depth, meaning, happiness, and most importantly love, into every aspect of our existence. We can deepen our experiences here on Earth just by incorporating a few of these truths into our lives.

Spirit *does* want us to experience rich, full, loving, beautiful lives here in our human bodies. We are asked to live and express love now, not simply to wait until our physical bodies die to experience it. They want us to live and love amazingly well, here and now, not put it on hold waiting for a reward later.

Some of these messages may seem familiar to you. Many have been a core part of religious and spiritual teachings for millennia. Why write about them again?

My Guide said that many of us here seem to have forgotten the basics. It's easy to get wrapped up in our day-to-day lives and forget that, at the core of each one of us, we really are loving, spiritual beings. Our souls are a part of God, and a part of God is in each one of us. Love, guidance, and blessings are there for us to access whenever we want or need. But sometimes we learn best when we hear or see things in a new way. A new format may have a different impact on us, so these insights are meant to help incorporate this knowledge into the modern world in a different way.

The messages are but one voice. For some of you, they may resonate and help your life become a little richer or more fulfilling. For others, some truths won't make much sense or won't feel right. That's OK and as it should be — not everyone learns in the same way, in the same time, or from the same source. I encourage you, though, to read through them and see how they *feel* to you. Perhaps even pick one at a time and work with it for as long as you need to, incorporating it into your life.

PRESENTING THE MESSAGES

Each message has its own chapter divided into a few main parts. First, I state the message itself as my Guide gave it to me. The "Full Message" section gives details as they were explained to me by my Guide. Each chapter also has a section called "My Thoughts" where I give a more human perspective on the message if I can. I'll also write about some of my own experiences in trying to make the message a part of my life. And for most chapters, I include some tips on putting that particular truth into practice.

You might notice that the "voice" of the text might change a little as you read through each chapter. The "Full Message" sections are written mostly from the viewpoint of my Guide. I've tried to make this content a bit more user-friendly and engaging, but it still might come across as more formal and stilted than my typical style. Remember, I was translating my Guide's communication of direct thought, feeling, and visual concepts; she actually *spoke* very few words. I did notice that the information she gave me seemed a bit stilted, as if she chose not to communicate in our current, informal style.

I wrote the "My Thoughts" section in each chapter from my own perspective, so you might notice that the wording is more natural, more modern, and more conversational. My Guide insisted that I add my own thoughts and experiences to this book. She expressed that it was important for me to be able to freely write about how this information has impacted me. These sections give a more human-centered view on the messages as well as suggestions as to how we might incorporate them into our lives. While definitely influenced by Spirit, I try as much as I can to bring in other viewpoints to make things clearer and easier to understand.

You might notice themes or a sense of repetition of concepts from one message to the next. This repetition is natural in that spiritual place because nothing exists in isolation. These truths connect together as the spoke-strands in a spiderweb. They form much of the structure and if you touch one of them, many of the rest reverberate in response. At first I had a difficult time trying to separate everything out in the way that my little scientist's brain felt was right, but then I realized there wasn't meant to be separation between the messages. They merge together and intertwine in a natural and fluid way.

Spiritual Communication

I'm not claiming that these messages came directly to me from Spirit. They didn't. My Guide acted as a relay. She explained that she spoke on behalf of many others, including Spirit. For my part, I am simply a recipient, messenger, and student. My Guide asked me to put this information out into the world to benefit anyone who feels drawn to read it, including me.

Communication came to me through my Guide in the form of concepts, visual images, and thoughts placed directly into my mind. Rarely did she pass on information to me verbally. The only time she did express herself with spoken words was when I didn't appear to understand her through one of the other communication methods. It seemed as though she would sometimes get a little stymied by my inability to understand her thoughts. When this happened she calmly switched to the communication method she knew I could easily comprehend.

At other times, it seemed as though she was simply helping me to remember all of this wisdom. It was already hidden somewhere deep in my own soul, buried under several layers of my humanity. I just needed someone to help me pull back the veil and remember.

I have tried to translate her communication into words as best as I could. In some instances, the language didn't materialize so I struggled to find a roughly equivalent term, hoping the meaning would come through. An example is the concept of love at the spiritual level. This was a very big feeling, heart-expanding, something so utterly large that my human experience could not fathom it. Trying to put this vast concept into words turned out to be impossible, so I did the best I could.

Why These Messages?

My Guide said that she and the other spiritual beings have seen that so many of us are unhappy or living unfulfilled lives. They want to help us so much but they struggle with how to reach us in ways that we can understand. They simply want us to see things here on Earth in a more loving and lighthearted way.

I understand. Before my accident, I felt that I didn't have much reason for *being*, that I hadn't really accomplished much and my future didn't seem very bright. I had a beautiful daughter, two wonderful sisters, and a few amazing and close friends. But I felt the rest of my life had stalled. I had turned my back on spiritual matters and love, but at the same time I wasn't really happy in that agnostic life I was living.

Perhaps it was time to bring me back into the fold, to teach me the things I needed to learn in order to live an amazing life. But it took a horrendous accident and a near-death experience for me to see the light. No matter how it happened, I am extremely grateful that I received these messages. I hope that you don't need to go through something quite that traumatic to gain some benefit through these words.

THE MESSAGES
The Messages themselves are short and deceptively simple:

1. We are not only on Earth to learn, but to Love
2. You are a miracle — treat yourself like one
3. This Earth and the universe are also miracles
4. Each one of us is more powerful than we imagine
5. Each one of us, all of Creation, is connected
6. Allow, let go, let Spirit work in your life
7. Show love to others by allowing them to show love
8. Learn to listen to your heart
9. You are never alone
10. Your most powerful tool is your power of choice
11. You have one chance at life as you — live fully
12. Live and feel your gratitude

The remainder of the chapters in this part of the book explain and discuss each message in more detail. The only recommendation I can give you is to read the first message on love before you dive in to the others. You don't need to read them all from start to finish, though. Each is a standalone chapter, so let your intuition guide you through the material. Your heart might ask you to linger on one longer than the others, or to skip around chapters randomly. Whatever seems right for you *will* be right for you.

You might learn something right away or the information might take some time to merge with your heart and mind. One or more of the messages might ring true for you while others don't seem to matter as much in this moment. Take away from this what you need, knowing that it's here for you whenever you need it.

This information is your birthright. It's not *my* wisdom. It's not something I've invented. This is a part of *our* spiritual wisdom, yours and mine. I'm just one of the people sent here to remind us of what we may have forgotten.

Even if you don't learn anything new, my wish is for you to come away with a renewed sense of enjoyment of being here on Earth and living this life that you have right now.

Life is truly a blessing.

CHAPTER 6

Love and Compassion

We are not on Earth to simply learn, but to love. We are on Earth to love everyone and everything. We are meant to find and experience joy in feeling and expressing love to others. It is through the acts of love and compassion that we are brought closer to our spiritual center, and to God.

Full Message

As I walked with my Guide through the landscape of my little corner of Heaven, the sense of a deep, loving presence flowed through everything. This sense still resonates with me, even back on Earth. The most difficult thing to give up when I came back to my body was that very tangible, ever-present, deep, powerful, and supportive love.

We often paused in our walk through Heaven just so I could revel in the ocean of love and peace flowing through me. On a hillside meadow, overlooking distant mountains, I let myself embrace that love while my Guide explained it to me.

She pointed out just how the power of love formed the structure of everything in Heaven. Standing there on that hillside, she allowed me to *see* the energy of love that existed at the core of everything there. It's tough to describe how one *sees* the vibration of love that exists at the heart of a tree, for example, but it was there, just below the surface. With her help, I experienced it fully.

It turns out that love is one of our main reasons for being on Earth. As love forms the structure of Heaven, it exists as an undercurrent in our world, too. While I was there, I saw and experienced this spiritual love as an undercurrent of intense, warm, all-encompassing energy that formed the structure of everything. Every tree, every mountain, every flower, and every cloud vibrated with love at its center. Now that I'm back in my regular life, I can sense that loving energy here on Earth too. It's all around us and when I allow myself to fully experience it, the feeling and sense of that love is overpowering in its beauty. I still get emotional when I allow myself to see and experience that love.

In reality, spiritual love is at the heart of *both* realms — Heaven and Earth. Love is meant to be a joy-filled expression of our connectedness to our Creator and to each other here on Earth.

It is through the *act* of love and being loving that we live fully.

Spiritual love doesn't mean loving just those people in our families, or simply loving people we agree with, but loving *everyone* and *everything*.

That's Big Love, and it's not always easy for us humans to live this way.

Each person has a spiritual spark inside. Each person is an expression of Divine love — not just those people we count as family or friends, but *everyone*. When we look into the eyes of another, we are also looking directly at Spirit. *Each person* is an expression of divinity, a window to the Creator, no matter the color of his skin, her religious affiliation, politics, or financial status. How could we *not* love each person we see, and thus love Spirit more fully through them?

God isn't simply asking us to love other people, but *all of* creation. The mountains, the air, the rain, the trees, the animals, and the stars are all connected spiritually. Nature and the universe aren't ours — they are loaned to us so that we may live beautiful lives, revel in creation, enjoy ourselves as humans, and practice love for all things. Loving creation in all of its forms demonstrates our gratitude to, and love for, Spirit and all that we have been given.

Besides being something we *feel*, love is also *an action we choose*.

Yes, it is our choice to *practice* love in some form or another every day. It isn't just an emotion that happens *to* us. We can choose to extend love, compassion, and kindness to everyone and everything in our lives. This may not be easy, but it's what we're being asked to do.

In choosing love, choosing *to love*, and choosing to open our hearts to see and experience love all around us, we will learn as well.

In choosing to love as expansively as we can, we will likely need to learn how to let go of past hurts and to see beyond the surface, straight to the heart of people or situations. Learning how to be vulnerable and compassionate is necessary, as is forgiving or letting go of the past. We will recognize the value of cooperation and the beauty of individuality, and that it is powerful to be a unique individual while at the same time allowing other people to be themselves.

In choosing to love, we choose to open ourselves to learning and living our lives fully as spiritual expressions.

Learning from Love

Practicing the action of love in all its forms teaches us to be vulnerable, generous, to show compassion to others, to ourselves, to the world, and to the universe. Actively demonstrating this love over time will teach us to be generous with our words and actions and to be compassionate with others, no matter their circumstances.

My Guide insisted that we try our best to extend love to everyone and everything on Earth: to you, your spouse or partner, friends, your siblings, the unfriendly neighbor down the street, the politician you don't agree with, those people across the sea that your country invaded last year, the folks with the skin color a shade or two different from your own, those who worship in a slightly different way from you, fans of the opposing team, and even the animals. All are a part of God and God loves all of them.

In extending love to everyone and everything, loving *all* of creation, we therefore love *all* of Spirit. Not just parts of Spirit as most of us do now. *All* of Spirit.

You Are Worthy of Your Own Love

Everything and everyone is connected spiritually. Try to look on all around you with love and appreciation for its tie to our Creator.

This means you, too.

You are a part of Spirit and there is a part of Spirit in you. The act of love I'm talking about also extends to you. Love yourself for the human and spiritual being that you are. Feel kindness and compassion for the person you are. Extend gratitude toward yourself as you would any other person.

Loving yourself unconditionally is one of the most precious gifts you can give back to God. In doing this, you are showing profound gratitude for one of Spirit's treasured creations — you!

Loving yourself means embracing both your light and dark sides. You may already embrace the light-filled part of your being. This is the part that you allow the world to see. The kind side, the compassionate part is the face that we feel comfortable showing to the world. But you have a darker side too (everyone does), and it also deserves your love, compassion, and kindness. The darker side is what you don't want the world to see, but it's also part of being human. Anger, jealousies, or telling lies can be part of our dark sides. But darkness is part of us. The only way to bring that dark side into the light, to change it into something you're proud to share, is to embrace it with your love. Extend compassion and kindness toward it. Allow it to morph into something beautiful, productive, or creative.

This loving of self is not an ego-driven, narcissistic love, but a truly compassionate, embracing love and kindness. Loving who and what you are means being gentle with yourself, but it also means feeling strength and making the tough choices when needed in your life. It means being willing to overcome, work through, or let go of your negative habits and fears, to treat yourself and your body with utmost respect, to feed it wholesome foods, to stay away from destructive substances, and to treat your body and mind as if it were Spirit's because in a very important way, it is.

You are a spiritual being — please start treating yourself like one.

If a spiritual master came to dinner at your house, what would you feed him or her? Would you feel good about serving cheap take-out pizza, fried chicken, corn chips, and overly processed cheese product? Or would you want to serve a home-cooked meal full of good, healthful food like salmon or a vegetarian entree, sweet potatoes, a salad, and some wonderful dark chocolate? Treat your own self as you would a spiritual master because at your heart, you are one.

Getting adequate exercise is also showing love to yourself. Remember how Jesus and Buddha traveled? They walked, constantly. Get out and walk, run, bike, swim, or whatever activity you enjoy. Use the gift of your body to its own highest potential. Appreciate it. Feel and love how all of the muscles, nerves, bones, ligaments, and tendons work in harmony to hike you up and down that hill, through the park, or along the edge of the canyon. Your body needs exercise in order to thrive.

Love yourself. Love *you* as a creation of Spirit.

Spirit will smile at you in return.

My Thoughts

The amount and intensity of love that I felt in Heaven is hard to put into words. Even now, when I talk about it with other people, the memory of that love often brings up deep emotions. It's still very powerful for me, partly because its message formed the core of the information I received and what I experienced. This one message could be the subject of an entire book on its own but in this volume, I try to narrow it down to its most basic, core components.

When I was in that "pre-Heaven," what struck me to my core was just how much love permeated everything. Love was everywhere. It formed the structure of all that surrounded me. Who could believe that loving energy could form the structure of things? But there, it did. I could feel its power radiating through everything: the landscape, the skies, the flowers, the clouds, and even me. The love that I sensed made me fall to my knees and weep with unbelievable joy. I was back in our spiritual home where we are all loved unconditionally. It's no wonder that I didn't notice my Guide until after I had felt that first rush of love wash through me. That God-level love was so all-consuming, welcoming, and perfect that I had difficulty concentrating on anything else.

I learned that one of the main reasons we're here on Earth is simple: to love. That's it. If that's all that you get from this book then you've understood its main message. Yes, we're here to enjoy our human selves, too, and perhaps even learn, but the heart of why we are here is love.

While the message sounds pretty simple, as humans it's not always easy to put into practice.

We're asked to love everyone regardless of their political persuasion, religious affiliation, their job title, annual income, skin color, age, and who they in turn love. Spirit asks that we put aside our differences and figure out some way to cherish and respect each other as the spiritual creations we are. It doesn't mean that we have to agree with everyone, but it does mean that through love and compassion, we work to overcome our differences and solve our problems, together, as one humanity.

It doesn't sound very easy, does it?

This doesn't mean to take everyone in to our homes or enter into a romantic relationship with them. We don't have to be friends with all who cross our paths. We don't even have to like everyone. What it does mean, though, is that we recognize other people fully for who they are:

someone who carries a spiritual spark of love at his or her core. It means that we show them respect, compassion, kindness, gentleness, and thus love.

It also means that we learn to extend that same love to ourselves.

No, this definitely isn't easy but it *is* our main reason for life, especially now when we face so much difficulty on this planet.

What is Love?

The concept of love is so vast that we might never come to an acceptable, working definition of it. I'll spare you from long, involved discussions on all of its components and will simply distill it down to its essential elements as I understand them right now.

I personally like the distinction the ancient Greeks used to describe love. They defined several types, including *agape*, *philia*, and *eros*.

Agape can be thought of as truly selfless, charitable, unconditional, deeply compassionate love. The New Testament equated *agape* with the spiritual love God feels toward humans, and I believe it's the kind of love that members of many religious faiths aspire to have toward others. In my view, true *agape* is not needful, selfish, childish, demanding, narcissistic, or controlling. It is very openhearted, deeply compassionate, and altruistic.

Does it sound intimidating? Let's move on to something a little more human, then.

Philia is a human feeling of "brotherly love." Think of it as pure, selfless, platonic love that you might feel for a friend and you're pretty close to understanding *philia*.

We can imagine *eros* as a feeling of love based in sexuality. I would guess that many of us adults are familiar with this.

On the other hand, Buddhism places large emphasis on both compassion and kindness. Compassion usually means "to have a deep feeling of sympathy and sorrow for another who is stricken with misfortune."[13]

---

13 www.Dictionary.com

Kindness is a friendly feeling, having a good disposition or generous attitude toward someone; being considerate, helpful, affectionate, or humane.

The kind of love I sensed coursing through me during my time in Heaven felt more akin to *agape*. It was a love that seemed to transcend the human experience. It was purely spiritual and probably isn't fully attainable by most people on Earth. But we can use the concept of *agape* as a starting point in defining what it is that we're being asked to do.

For myself, I try to combine the concepts of *agape*, *philia*, kindness, and compassion to come up with the idea for the type of love that I aspire to. This is what I want to give to the people and world around me. I'm not a saint and I'm far from perfect, so pure *agape* is likely beyond my reach. But I can aspire to it, just as I can aspire to be kind and compassionate to everyone and everything.

In my life now, I start by treating people with kindness and compassion, then add in some brotherly love and as much *agape* as I can given my human, and thus non-perfect, nature. Some might call this combined concept *loving-kindness*, and that's an easy way to think of it.

The takeaway from this is to do the best we can. Be kind as much as possible. Feel compassionate toward others more often than not. Extend some brotherly love, and aspire to *agape* when possible.

Any definition of *love* is flawed in a way. As in Tao ("the Tao that can be named is not the Tao"), so the love that we name here is not the *feeling* of love we're talking about. It's tough to define and any human definition of love doesn't do justice to love itself.

Just thinking of love as that sense of deep, selfless affection, caring, and compassion for another, and for all around us, will put you on a path to understanding it for yourself.

Active Loving

I learned that love is active and not attached to conditions. We just *love*, regardless of externals. This is *agape*, described above. I may not agree with what another person does or stands for, but extending kindness and compassion to him as a part of Spirit is what I'm being asked to do.

This active loving was a new concept for me but it made sense when I saw it demonstrated. My Guide didn't necessarily like some of my life's choices up to that point. She made this quite clear. But that didn't stop her from extending love to me. She encircled me with her love and compassion almost continually while I walked with her. I felt her understanding of the difficulties we all face here on Earth, and she wanted us all to know that we are still actively loved.

This is the love that Jesus taught when he walked this Earth. It's also the love that Buddha taught, and St. Francis too. It is the love and compassion that we, in turn, should try to extend to everyone. We often choose to withhold it or aren't capable of giving it because of our upbringing, fears, pathologies, anger, misunderstandings, or experience.

Ultimately, though, we're supposed to put the excuses aside, work through our internal blocks and just start practicing love, kindness, and compassion a bit more.

Simple, but definitely not always easy.

I think many of us recognize that humanity is at a point where we really *do* need to learn to love each other. The good news is that we can actually make it happen. To choose not to even try, though, is not OK. No one is perfect, no one will ever be able to love 100%, but we can try. We can do our best. That's all Spirit asks for.

We can no longer afford to ignore, or worse, hate, other people based on arbitrary lines drawn on a map, or which door they walk through on Saturday or Sunday. My Guide asked us to come together as a planet of intelligent, compassionate, loving beings. It's time to recognize that each person is just as valuable as any other no matter their continent, skin tone, or language. Seeing the Spirit within each person, and respecting that each person may call God by a different name is the goal we're asked to work toward. Some may not even recognize "Spirit," and that's OK too. Our job is to respect and love our differences as humans, revel in them, but still learn to work together to create something amazing here on Earth.

We can. I've seen what we all are at our cores: amazing, love-filled beings of light and compassion. Our future depends on our ability to perceive this inner spiritual being inside each and every person, and in learning to cohabit this planet in a more loving, mature, and cooperative way.

In learning to love each other, we learn about many other things too, such as how to communicate in loving ways, how to let go and move on, how to release our stringent attachments to "the way things should be," and even how to treat ourselves with care and respect. Through learning to love others, we can learn to love ourselves.

In the words of my Guide:

> *"We know that it is easy for you to show love to others when a disaster strikes. So many of you rise to help during times of crisis: a flood, an earthquake, a severe fire. While we salute you for helping others in these times, for showing love during a crisis, the world needs your love all of the time, not just during a disaster. Helping others on a normal day is just as powerful and necessary an act of love as helping out disaster victims every few years.*
>
> *Do not wait for a disaster to strike to show your love and caring to others. After all, Spirit does not wait for tough times to show love and caring to you. Spiritual love surrounds you all of the time, every day, every night, in good times, and in bad. Try to emulate this pattern in yourself, with those around you. Give love, BE love as much as you can. Your world will be a better place for your efforts."*

Loving Those We Don't Like

How do we extend love to people we don't like, or whose views or beliefs are abhorrent to us? How can we extend love, of all things, to people we might view as bullies, criminals, or terrorists?

Let's drop the word *love* for now and replace it with concepts that are easier to apply to others: deep compassion and kindness.

Compassion and kindness as synonyms for love was the view that many spiritual masters taught, and continue to teach (Jesus, the Buddha, the Dalai Lama, etc.). And these masters taught that I can extend compassion and kindness to everyone.

Extending compassion doesn't mean that I must *like* the other person, agree with what they stand for, *or condone what they do.* In the case of people who harm others, I definitely don't agree with them or their actions. However, I do have compassion for them in: how they were raised; their family and culture of origin; irrational fears inherited from parents or society; possible personality, mental, or emotional disorders; and any extreme religious or political views they were immersed in from childhood. I have compassion for them misunderstanding the words of whatever spiritual text they follow, or falling victim to a charismatic but ego-driven leader.

But extending compassion to people who hurt others doesn't mean we need to allow those bullies to continue. In the case of terrorists, I have deep compassion for the people they are terrorizing, the families of victims, and the world as well. Terrorists are perhaps not much different at their cores from serial murderers here in the USA, except that they are much more visible about it. Terrorists are bullies on a very large scale. While I feel a base level of compassion for bullies, I will also be the first one to stand up against one as well (and have, many times).

And standing up to bullies, terrorists, or any other form of darkness is also compassionate — for them and for the people they are victimizing. Sometimes when I confront bullies, it forces them to face their actions, realize they've been not-so-kind, and gives them a chance to make changes. At the very least, in the case of murderers, locking them up and giving them opportunities at rehabilitation is extremely loving and compassionate. They may choose not to face their dark sides or change their destructive behaviors, but we've at least given them the chance to do so. And we're also protecting those who might become future victims.

Let's not forget that almost every society has allowed or perpetrated horrendous, violent acts against others. And I have compassion for others experiencing this now because we in the USA have also gone through it. In the past, the USA has perpetrated state- or religious-sanctioned acts of terror, genocide, and violence on others. Do I like this? No. Do I condone what we did? No. And the fact that my country has participated in this doesn't make it right for others to do it now. *It's never right.* It's not loving or compassionate. But it happened, and I can use it as a starting point to understand why it continues to happen in almost every society.

I wonder if many of us realize we're not so very different from *them* even now, and it scares us. We're not terribly removed from that darkness in our own pasts, so seeing it on the nightly news is an uncomfortable reminder of where we came from.

Terrorism and genocide of one flavor or another haunts human history. That doesn't mean we give in to it, though. I believe humanity is slowly evolving away from this dark undercurrent, but it will take a lot of time and a lot of people standing up against the bullying and terror for it to stop. The key is not allowing ourselves to fall into the trap of becoming that which we stand against.

Be a voice for what you want to see in the world. Be the change you want to see in the world.[14]

Is turning the other cheek and letting someone abuse you again, compassionate? Not in my opinion. It's not compassionate or respectful to you, nor is it compassionate for the other person. Standing up against a bully is compassionate. But standing up against him doesn't mean that you assault him, degrade him, or do the same things back to him. It could mean saying, "It's not cool to pick on someone smaller than you," or taking action that demonstrates, "It's not cool to use terror to get what you want."

---

14 Mahatma Ghandi

Being compassionate and loving could mean setting a boundary and not accepting the abusive behavior anymore. It could mean telling a friend that her behavior toward others is abusive and you can't hang around her anymore if she continues. This may be the wake-up call she needs to take a look at her words and actions. We can do these things gently and with compassion, both in our own lives and on the world stage.

The Gem of Love

As my Guide and I stood on the hillside in Heaven, I had a hard time grasping the cosmic enormity of love. I could feel it as a force, but I couldn't wrap my mind around its extent. Since I'm a visual person, my Guide chose to show me a visual of the concept of deep, spiritual love.

An image formed in front of me, somehow superimposed over the distant mountains. I saw God's love as an unimaginably huge, gleaming diamond, one so big that I couldn't see from one edge to the other. The surface of the diamond was cut into infinite facets, each one sparkling and reflecting a small part of the light emanating from the whole. Love for a spouse was one facet on the surface of that huge diamond — it sent out its own sparkle but was also part of the larger array of love that came from the diamond as a whole. Love for a child was another facet, and so on. Together, these little bits of human love were the sparkle on the surface of the bigger gem of spiritual love.

Ahhh, now I understood. And as soon as I understood the analogy, the vision disappeared.

Loving Ourselves

My Guide then turned to me and said, "We see that you often treat your pets much better than you treat yourselves!"

I felt her profound sadness, but it was tinged with a little humor, too. How many of us truly love ourselves? How many of us accept both our dark and light sides with compassion? How many of us look in the mirror and see a spiritual being staring back at us in our reflection?

Yes, our pets do deserve our love, but each of us deserves to have the love, compassion, and kindness of at least one person: ourselves. Unfortunately, loving ourselves may be the hardest task of all. It's easy to direct love outward. Try to channel it inward, though, and you risk dredging up long-buried, painful emotions and memories that prefer to hide out in the darkness. In order for these memories to heal, they need the light of love shed on them, and specifically they need our own love.

What is your self-talk like? In my own life, I now gauge my level of compassion for myself by paying attention to what's rattling around in my mind. If it's positive overall, that means I'm feeling a good amount of compassion and kindness for myself. If it's equal amounts positive and negative, I think about why that is and work on feeling more compassion to myself. And if the self-talk is mostly negative, I know it's time to direct much more kindness and compassion internally.

When we love ourselves in a very open, healthy, non-judgmental way, we also direct gratitude and love back to Spirit for the gift of life we have been given. When we love ourselves, we love the spark that Spirit has put inside each one of us.

Spirit understands that for many of us, loving ourselves is difficult. Try to feel compassion, kindness, and gratitude for who you are.

It may be easier to love an enemy, but loving ourselves is something we should make a priority. In the end, if we can learn to love ourselves unconditionally, loving everyone around us will be easier.

Turning Lack into Love

In the months before my accident, I had developed a very negative viewpoint on love. I occasionally saw evidence of love such as in the lives of a few friends who seemed to have found their respective soulmates. I felt a tad jealous but happy for them at the same time, all the while thinking that kind of love could never happen in my life. I wanted it, but I didn't know how to get it so I focused on its absence, not its abundance.

I didn't have anyone special romantically, and while I had some very good, close friends and loving family members, I certainly didn't feel *surrounded by* love.

The negativity on the nightly news skewed my thoughts too, and I came away with a rather gloomy outlook of my fellow humans.[15] Why couldn't people just put aside their differences and love each other, or at least care enough about each other to stop the violence, the killing, the abuse, the stealing, etc.? The ignorance and suffering of violence bothered me a lot. It still does, but at that time I used it to justify my grim outlook on life and love.

I bet it comes as no surprise then to learn that just before my accident, I wasn't the happiest person in the world. Focusing on the lack of love around me effectively made that come true in my life. It's all I could see.

In those months before the accident, I had difficulty spending time with others and making new friends because of my increasingly negative outlook. It pushed people away rather than created a space for them to come closer. Even though pushing people away is not what I wanted, my attitude put a barrier up between me and any possibility of a friendship from the start.

I pushed *all* forms of love away before it had a chance to get started. Why? Because I hadn't yet learned to *truly* love myself.

My experience during surgery changed all of this.

---

15 I've actually shied away from watching the news on TV. Now I prefer to read the news online — it's easier for me to pick and choose the stories I expose my mind to this way.

During my NDE, the amount of love in that spiritual place overwhelmed me — I saw it everywhere. It made up everything. It seemed to be the creative force of existence. More importantly, I *felt* it deep inside of my body and soul and the feeling of it put me in such a blissfully ecstatic state that I was on the verge of tears the entire time I was there. For the first time in my life I truly felt unconditional love being directed at me. And I felt it for myself, too.

There was nowhere that love was *not*.

True *agape*.

I felt the love that God had for me. I was loved simply for being me, and Spirit loves all of us here on Earth just for being us. There is no one that is not included in this love. We are loved beyond our ability to measure it.

This spiritual love became an example for me. After my experience, I understood that I was being challenged to extend love, compassion, and kindness to everyone, just as spiritual love is there for everyone right now.

When I came back to my body, at first I felt a bit let down because the love wasn't as obvious. Seeing the love around me proved difficult at first, with my broken body hooked up to IVs and monitors. But once the initial shock of being Nancy again wore off[16], I was able to partially return to that enraptured state of experiencing and seeing love all around. And I noticed that I really did love me, too. I loved my determination, my strength, and even my broken bones. I felt compassion for my own frustration with my pain. And then something amazing happened — the more I directed love to myself, the more I saw it in the world around me.

In time, I was able to see how much my family and friends loved me. I had not fully noticed the depth of their love before, but now it was apparent. My family members and a friend put their lives aside for a time to come help me heal. They assisted me with the most menial chores of daily living. You name it, they did it, with love.

---

16 In Heaven, I didn't really have a name *per se*, I was simply me. I was different, yet part of the whole of Creation too. I was unique and had an identity that went beyond words and beyond a name.

Many, many days I cried tears of deep gratitude for being the recipient of their love.

My coworkers organized a cooking brigade. For about six weeks, they took turns cooking meals and buying food for me and my family. During my recovery process, coworkers even helped with menial tasks such as moving things out of my home and into my garage to make maneuvering easier in my less-mobile state.

This was their way of showing love and support. Again, many times I choked back tears from seeing and feeling all of the love and concern they put into their efforts to help.

I saw the love that medical professionals gave to their patients every day. Many of them love what they do and pour every ounce of that into their patients, but it often goes unappreciated or unseen.

Love residing in people from all walks of life became obvious to me. I saw love in the chaplains, the housekeepers, the nursing assistants, in the paramedics, in the therapists, and in the food service workers. I could finally sense the love at the core of their beings and it helped me feel good about being back here in this world. Even if people didn't intend to let others see that love burning inside of them, I could see it now. Sensing their love made me blissfully happy.

A few weeks after the accident I was able to start walking outside again and the love that made up the world became obvious. I felt it here just as I did in Heaven. Spiritual love felt more subtle on Earth, a bit more hidden, but it ran through everything and everyone: animals, plants, landscapes, the mountains, the prairies, the rivers, the oceans. The world sung with a chorus of loving energy and my heart reverberated in joy at finally hearing, seeing, and feeling this song!

And in rare moments, the sheer amount of love I felt overwhelmed me, sometimes to the point of tears.

I still carry this blissful feeling with me. I see love all around now where I only wanted to see its absence before. Love flows through everything, and everyone, no matter our outward religion, our marital status, our skin color, or what country we live in. Spirit loves us too, all of us. There is not a one of us that is closed off.

In my own life, I love and appreciate myself more deeply than I have at any time in the past. What I feel isn't an arrogant or narcissistic love, rather it's a sense of deep compassion and kindness for the person I am in this life. I enjoy the mix of talents, interests, and quirky character traits that make up who I am. I'm beginning to embrace any darkness within me and work at bringing it into the light. I'm deeply happy within myself, possibly for the first time since I was a young child. New friends have come along. Most longtime friends are still in my life. I smile and laugh a lot now because my heart is lighter from knowing this love. I am allowing the kinder, calmer, gentler, more loving side of my nature to take over, and the negativity and pessimism is put on the back burner.

It's about time!

1 Corinthians 13:1-13 (NIV)

If I speak in the tongues of men or of angels, but do not have love, I am only a resounding gong or a clanging cymbal. If I have the gift of prophecy and can fathom all mysteries and all knowledge, and if I have a faith that can move mountains, but do not have love, I am nothing. If I give all I possess to the poor and give over my body to hardship that I may boast, but do not have love, I gain nothing.
Love is patient, love is kind. It does not envy, it does not boast, it is not proud. It does not dishonor others, it is not self-seeking, it is not easily angered, it keeps no record of wrongs. Love does not delight in evil but rejoices with the truth. It always protects, always trusts, always hopes, always perseveres.
Love never fails. But where there are prophecies, they will cease; where there are tongues, they will be stilled; where there is knowledge, it will pass away. For we know in part and we prophesy in part, but when completeness comes, what is in part disappears. When I was a child,

I talked like a child, I thought like a child, I reasoned like a child. When I became a man, I put the ways of childhood behind me. For now we see only a reflection as in a mirror; then we shall see face to face. Now I know in part; then I shall know fully, even as I am fully known.
And now these three remain: faith, hope and love. But the greatest of these is love.

Practice Love

What does it mean when Spirit asks us to extend love to everyone? What does that look like in practice? Here are some ideas that I use for exercising my ability to feel love, compassion, and kindness for everyone:

- *I look into the eyes of a child, preferably my own, and try to see the spark of the Divine inside him or her.* That little person looking back at me is a part of God. I try to see and feel that as deeply as I can. I feel gratitude in my heart for that Divine nature inside my child.
- *I do the above exercise with my partner or a close friend (if you're married, you can do this exercise with your spouse).* I look into his or her eyes, seeing the spiritual light right there in front of me. He or she is a part of Spirit too, and I try to feel grateful for being able to see this. I see the love shining back at me — a facet of that gem of spiritual love, *agape*. I allow that feeling to glow in my heart, then I express my thanks and appreciation and love back to my partner or friend.
- *I practice finding the spark of Spirit inside people I encounter in a normal day.* I don't necessarily need to stare into their eyes — this might freak them out! I simply look at their faces, smile, and realize that they have a spiritual core too. Spirit is inside of them. If you want to try this for yourself, I recommend starting with friends, acquaintances, coworkers, and people you know or like. Then later, try it

out on people you don't necessarily like: perhaps a supervisor at work, a crabby taxi or bus driver, or your former spouse.

- *In a quiet moment, I take time to contemplate one person at random from my day.* I think about what that person can teach me about God and about love. For example, if the person that comes to mind is an energetic teenager, I might see his unbridled love for life in how he throws himself into a sport.
- *Again, I take some quiet time and contemplate someone from my day who I don't necessarily like or agree with.* What can I learn from that person? What can I learn about Spirit? Is that person present in my life to teach me something about myself, perhaps something I don't want to see? Can I at least feel a sense of kindness or compassion for that person? I feel gratitude for having that person in my life and for the lessons he or she is teaching me.
- *I practice finding the good in people, including myself.* The vast majority of people are not *all* bad, no matter what our human brains might try to tell us. Contemplating someone I had a conflict with forces me to look below the surface for the good, the spark of Spirit. What good can I find in that person? What can I see in him or her that is loving? Can I find something in that person to admire, respect, like, or enjoy? Does she rescue abused animals in her spare time, or perhaps help run a homeless shelter on the weekends? Does he treat his kids well, or help others to grow gorgeous and fruitful gardens? Do they help build homes for families in need? Finding those little gems inside each person helps me see their spiritual centers. Once I have found one or more of those gems, I try to feel gratitude for that person's presence in my life.
- *Taking a walk in nature, even if "nature" is a small city park, helps me reconnect to love.* While walking, I spend a few minutes quietly considering the nature around me — the birds singing, the blue sky, the grasses, the trees, the flowers, even the blades of grass

pushing up through cracks in the sidewalk. Whatever I see, I think about its inner spiritual spark and practice seeing it as a creation of God.

* *I often go on what I call Love Walks.* This activity really connects me to Spirit and love. I take a walk through my town and look for any evidence of love that I can find. Perhaps I spot an elderly couple walking together hand-in-hand, still obviously in love after a lifetime together. Or I might see an older sibling helping a younger sibling learn how to play basketball. Maybe I notice a young mother cradling her newborn in a loving embrace, or a small boy hugging his four-legged best friend. Perhaps I see a baby deer being protected and nursed by its mother. I just automatically feel grateful for having witnessed these signs of love, and feel gratitude for this gift you've been given — the gift of seeing others practice love.

CHAPTER 7

You Are A Miracle

You are a miracle. Treat yourself like one in all you do, say, and think. You have been given the glorious gifts of your life, your body, and your mind. Use these gifts fully, with joy.

Full Message

Heaven was, and is, a miraculous place. Everything seemed overflowing with love, joy, and peace. When I returned to my life on Earth, it seemed mundane somehow and paled in comparison to the richness of Heaven. But my Guide and the beings who communicated through her wanted us all to know just how much of a miracle we have in this life, no matter how routine or mundane it may seem. Each one of our lives is miraculous.

Images of mothers giving birth, of fathers holding their children, kids playing sports, and adults falling in love were placed in my mind by my Guide as she walked with me in Heaven. We walked through a grove of trees and images of a mother and father cradling a newborn flooded my mind. Then it was an elderly woman helping her grandson read a story, or a young couple on their wedding day.

What I learned is that we on Earth have something that those in Heaven don't: the gift of life. Each one of us is a miracle, a gift. You too are a miracle!

Every one of us is a beautiful, glorious, Spirit-filled person here to enjoy life, experience and give love, and help each other along our individual paths. No matter our skin color, language, height, eye color, and abilities, each one of us has a spark of Divine greatness built inside. We don't have to rule a country or be a billionaire to be great. *Great* in Spirit's eyes means living as fully, lovingly, joyfully, and compassionately as possible. It means living this gift as much as we can.

Doing big deeds in service to Spirit, our fellow humans, and the Earth is *great*. *Great* can also be shoveling our elderly neighbor's sidewalk free of snow when no one is looking. It can be entering a profession that heals the sick because we know down deep inside that is our calling. *Great* can be teaching disadvantaged children how to read because of the positive influence it has on their lives. It can also be volunteering to rescue and heal injured animals, or founding a charity that helps the poor. It can include showing others the path to health and fitness, or being a role model for at-risk teens.

My Guide put it to me this way:

> *"Each of you has a unique set of attributes, talents, and personality traits that makes you unique, and yes, even 'great.' Your greatness, your purpose, is individual and built inside of you. It can be any of the things mentioned above, or something completely different than what I can even dream up. No one can tell you what your purpose is, though. You need to find it in yourself."*

We on Earth have gifts that those in Heaven don't: the miraculous gifts of our lives, bodies, and minds allow us to have large, positive impacts on our world. We can enjoy fun in this physical realm, too: have families, ski a mountain slope, experience a full range of human emotions, take a deep breath of fresh air, and laugh at a horrible joke. We can build a home or a city, fly to the moon, invent a new technology, cure a disease, or lend help to those in need. We can do so much if we just understand how amazing we each are!

You are a gift. You are a miracle. When are you going to treat yourself like one?

So many of us never understand how special we really are. We are each a miraculous gift from Spirit. Each one of us has the power to live a fulfilled, amazing life. Each one of us has the potential to positively impact the world.

Those in Heaven want us to see just how amazing we are.

Care for Yourself

What do you feed your body? How do you keep your mind bright and youthful? Caring for yourself is a way to gift love, kindness, and compassion on *you*.

One excellent way to show our gratitude for this life we have is to treat ourselves well. Learn to love and respect your body by drinking clean water, eating healthy foods, getting the right amount of exercise for you, and spending time in the fresh air and sunshine.

God wants you to enjoy your life. Go for a walk, a run, or a bicycle ride to revel in movement. Swim in a clean lake and enjoy the feel of the cool water. Stand on the top of a hill or mountain and throw your arms back in celebration of life.

Love your body with fun, healthy, and challenging experiences. Feed your brain with good books, media, movies, and information. Try to avoid things that distress your mind because they also stress your body. Love your brain with challenging, new experiences, good people, and healthy hobbies and habits. Allow your creativity to shine through, whatever it is, for it is also a gift.

Each person is unique, with individual combinations of talents, abilities, likes, dislikes, strengths, and weaknesses. Live life as fully as you can. When you enjoy and appreciate who you are, that sends a big "Thank You" back to Spirit. In this way you graciously *live* your gratitude for your life. Have fun discovering who you really are, then live life to the best of your abilities.

Each one of us has at least one aspect that is truly special, something we can share with those around us that might bring a little joy or light into the world. We are each creative in our own way — a little bit of that spiritual creativity exists inside each of us. Do you know what your creative gifts are?

Follow your heart to discover what that creativity is. You may have just one form of expression, maybe four, but pay attention to them and cultivate them. Exercising those creative sparks is a way of thanking Spirit for your gifts. Leaving them unused or ignored is a quiet way of telling Spirit that you're not grateful for the talents you have.

Your forms of creativity may include drawing, painting, decorating a home, creating nutritious meals, restoring old cars, growing a garden, building furniture, or architecting a skyscraper. Your talents might lie in singing, dancing, photography, writing, computer programming, or building homes. Any of these things, and many more, can embody your spark of creativity.

You deserve to treat yourself with love, compassion, respect, and kindness. Others too deserve to be treated this same way. Looking upon each other as the miracles that we are is a wonderful way to show gratitude back to Spirit for everyone around us.

The gift of being human is precious. Love yourself. Love the miracle that is you. Start treating yourself with love and respect and see if your world changes for the better.

THE MIRACLES AROUND YOU

Every other person is a miracle too — the people we love, yes, but also the people we might not like so much. When we look into the eyes of any other person, we are looking straight into the eyes of Spirit, directly into the soul of another miracle. Whether a friend or enemy, each person around us is invested and infused with Spirit. Each person has the spark of the Creator inside. Each person is miraculous.

Think about this: what words do you use when you talk to the co-worker you don't get along with very well? How about your spouse, your neighbor, the cab driver, the bagel-cart vendor? Do you treat them all with respect, compassion, and kindness, or do you treat them with disdain, impatience, and a sharp tongue? It might help to think about each person that our lives touch as being a Jesus, Buddha, Muhammad, or a saint in disguise.

We can try to remember that each person has something to show us about ourselves or teach us about the world. Each person truly can be a mirror, a messenger, or a teacher for us if we choose to think about it in this way.

Power of Words

Our words hold energy and power whether we speak them aloud to others or silently to ourselves. What words do you use when you speak to yourself? How do you think about or speak to others?

Words spoken aloud can have power in the life of another. We can lift someone up or tear them down simply with the words we choose to speak. Therapists' offices are filled with the adult children of verbally abusive parents. My Guide cautions us to be thoughtful in our choice of words — it's possible to get our feelings across to someone without tearing him or her apart. It might help to keep in mind that the person staring back at us, the one we might be about to verbally attack, is a spiritual being too.

Would we berate Jesus or Buddha in the way we sometimes berate our child? Would we cut down God in the same way we just cut down our spouse? Or would we be gentle, using non-judgmental words in a way that still gets our point across while not attacking the other? Spirit knows that our human emotions can be strong, but strong emotion does not give us free reign to belittle and possibly damage someone else.

Even more, my Guide truly didn't understand why we turn those damaging words inward and talk to ourselves in the same disparaging way. Remember that when we use our words to tear ourselves apart internally, we're hurting ourselves.

Words carry power whether directed outward or inward. They can damage or heal. They can degrade or make someone's spirits soar. It is your choice which to use. It is your choice whether to lift someone up or tear them apart, including you. Use words that speak to the miracle that you are.

MY THOUGHTS

We're all glorious beings. Billions of cells of different types come together in you and, for the majority of us, work pretty well for many years to give us this time on Earth. We don't have to think about our cells functioning to stay alive. Our bodies tend to go about the daily aspects of living without much intervention from us. We breathe, our hearts beat, and we digest our food without thought. Most of the time, our physical wounds heal with little help. Our bodies just *know* how to heal. We get a scrape or scratch and in about ten days, new skin has formed and the scrape is gone. If we break a bone, we might have it set but after that our bodies start to knit the broken pieces back together, sometimes with the healed bone being stronger than it was before the break. We don't have to think "heal, heal, heal" every day. Our bodies just do it.

Our bodies replicate and replace old, tired cells with new ones. In this way we're constantly regenerated. Most of us can fairly easily create new versions of ourselves in the form of children who will carry a little bit of us into the future.

We can sing (some of us better than others), say "I love you," and give speeches that move nations to overcome great challenges. We can play the violin, run a marathon, or swim the English Channel. Our minds have engineered ways to send humans to the moon and spacecraft outside of our solar system.

Think of the gifts of our senses. Our noses and brains can tell the difference between a rose and a lily just by a single sniff. With our sense of touch, we can distinguish between the softness of a newborn's skin and the rough surface of sandpaper. We can hear both the song of the meadowlark nearby and the roar of a jet taking off from the airport in the distance. Our mouths can taste the faint sweetness of honeysuckle nectar and the sour taste of fresh lemon. And our eyes can take in a glorious sunset or the smile on our child's face when she looks at her new puppy.

Our senses tell us not only about the world, but they can speak to us about ourselves too. Would you rather listen to the dawn chorus of birds or a church choir on a Sunday morning? Do you dislike the taste of asparagus, and think the smell of a skunk isn't all that bad? Those are things that help define who you are in this life.

And then there is you — the whole person. Beautiful, glorious you.

Yes, you are the sum of all of these individual components, but you are so much more than that too. And your spiritual source wants you to know how amazing you are, just as you are right now.

We can always improve, but we are each one of us a wonder, simply as we are.

Our lives are tremendous gifts and it saddened my Guide that so many of us take ourselves for granted or don't appreciate ourselves as much as we could. We might hate ourselves, feel shame about our bodies, have self-destructive behaviors, use street drugs that put us in danger, eat poorly, drink too much alcohol, or even choose not to live the biggest and best life possible. We deny our creativity, intelligence, beauty, physical abilities, and inner strength.

Most adults have the capability to live much better and much larger lives than we currently live. Often we allow others to dictate to us what we should do based on their own dysfunctions and fears. We allow society or religions to tell us what profession to enter instead of following the calling in our hearts. We wallow in the shame and guilt that were pressed on us during childhood. We allow the past to haunt our present by giving it too much weight and hanging on to it for dear life rather than letting it go. We let irrational or non-existent fears to make our decisions for us.

Any of these things can keep us from living our best lives.

We are asked to work to stop the negative things we're doing inside our minds and see ourselves as the miracles that we truly are. Once we believe in our own miraculous natures, our lives will improve in amazing ways.

Each one of us is just as special as someone we might consider "great." We just don't realize it or don't acknowledge it as a truth.

The message is that we each need to do what it takes to overcome our own learned and self-perpetuated inadequacies, our own fears, and our own judgments in order to live the amazing lives Spirit would love for us to live.

If that means working through every self-help book on the shelf at your local bookstore, do it. If that means seeking psychotherapy, do it. If that means joining discussion groups in your church on living a more fulfilled life, do it. Do whatever it takes, because you deserve to create a fulfilling life for yourself.

That's not easy, is it? And it may take years of work for someone to release those mental or emotional blocks. In hindsight, I think my Guide understood the difficulties in coming to love ourselves so also wanted us to try it another way. Take baby steps. Just choose one way to treat yourself better. Maybe it's going for a 15 minute walk when the weather is nice. Perhaps it's choosing to eat only healthful food for one meal today. Take one small step in treating yourself better. Then next week, add another step on to the first.

See where those baby steps take you.

Practice Seeing Miracles

Seeing miracles around me is really an extension of the exercises on love in the previous chapter. Below are some additional ways that I see miracles around me:

- *I Practice finding the spark of the Divine inside people I encounter during my day.* I look into the eyes of another person and remember that somewhere inside is a little bit of the Divine. I feel grateful for that spark. If you want to try this exercise yourself, I'd recommend starting with someone you know and love to make it easier.
- *I find a mirror, look into it, and stare deeply into my own eyes.* I look for the spark of Spirit there, inside of me. This can be very difficult and I sometimes get emotional, but the results are worth it. I come away seeing myself as a part of Spirit, and the gives me renewed faith, hope, and energy in my own life.
- *Now to that reflection of you in the mirror, I say: You are worthy. You are special. You are a miracle.* I repeat until I start to believe it, even a little bit. I allow any emotions to surface. As this gets more comfortable, I change what I say to: I am worthy. I am special. I am a miracle.[17]
- *I do a self-care check-in: how well am I taking care of my body?* Can I improve the quality of my food? Do I need to acquire more good self-care habits and give up some negative ones? Do I need to visit my doctor for a physical?
- *How is my exercise?* Do I need to do more or change what I'm doing? Do I need to get outside, into the sun and fresh air?
- *Am I taking time out of my day for myself, even if it's only for five or ten minutes?*
- *What are my dreams for myself, what are my heart-callings?* If I don't know, I devote some quiet times of reflection to this. What have I always wanted to do? (If you need a nudge, the book *Second Acts* by Stephen M. Pollan is wonderful at helping you figure out what your dreams for yourself might be, and how to achieve them.)
- *I write down as many small steps as I can think of that I can take to advance myself in the direction of my dreams.* It's sometimes easier to take many small steps through life than one large one. When

---

[17] If you experience too much uncomfortable emotion or a severe reaction to this exercise, please stop. Consult with a trusted advisor, chaplain, or mental health professional for advice or treatment.

I managed large technology-based projects, this is exactly the method we used to meet impossible-sounding deadlines. I can apply a similar technique to advancing myself toward my dreams in my own life. What steps do you need to take to advance toward your goals?

- *Then I aim to take at least one of those small steps each week.*
- *I spend at least five minutes a day in contemplative silence or meditation.* My inner wisdom speaks to me best during quiet times, so the more I can cultivate quiet in my life, the more chances I have to hear it. If you want to try this, start by sitting quietly in a room with no distractions. Breathe in and out, deeply into your belly. Think the words "in" as you inhale and "out" as you exhale (this helps quiet the mind). Then when you're feeling quiet inside, silently ask yourself what you need to see or know at this moment in time. If something pops into your mind or inner vision, take note of it so that you can deal with it later.
- *I think about the words I direct toward myself. Are these words helping me or hurting me?* Would I speak them to my mother, my sister, or my best friend? If the answer is that my own words are hurting me, and I wouldn't speak them to someone I loved, I pay more attention to my self-talk. I become mindful of my own words, and let go of the need to tear myself apart.

CHAPTER 8

Earth is a Miracle

THE WORLD IS A MIRACLE *that we enhance with every thought, word, and action.*

FULL MESSAGE

"Listen to the voice of nature for it holds treasures for you."
~ Huron wisdom

My Guide and the beings who spoke through her showed me how much they revere their world, Heaven. They often reminded me of their love for their realm by allowing me to feel it as I strolled through that peaceful landscape. It's their home, one they love beyond measure.

As my Guide led me on my tour, she allowed me to feel her love for Heaven. Her emotions seemed to cause flowers to change color. I felt her joy and laughter come into my own heart when she looked up at the sky and saw rabbits and dragons disguised as clouds. And I felt her own sense of peace and belonging as she closed her eyes and allowed the gentle breezes to flow over her skin.

As she allowed me to feel these with her, she communicated to me the message she wanted us all to hear. She hoped that we could love our own home, Earth, as much as she loves hers. It might be easier to do if we think of Earth as an expression of spiritual love in physical form. While Earth has a physical presence and a history of its own, it also is our only home in this grand universe, the place we've been given for our life as humans.

We have been given the gift of the Earth but ultimately it doesn't belong to us. We can't really own it — each of our lifetimes are too short when compared to the life of the Earth to truly think of it as *ours*. We are transients in a way. We live here for maybe 75 to 100 years, then we're gone, leaving what once was our home for the next generations to care for.

Earth belongs to *itself*. It also belongs to those humans and animals who will come after us, as well as Spirit. It's here for us to live, play in life, experience love, and share in a deeper spiritual connection. It nourishes our bodies with the food we grow on it; it energizes our souls through its beautiful vistas; it gives us shelter, a place to call home in this vast galaxy we call the Milky Way.

We can't live without it.

Through living in the physical world, we can come to know nature's beauty, then connect more deeply to our spiritual centers through that beauty: the blush of the sunset over the mountains, the joy of seeing a young eagle take its first flight, the grandeur of vast canyons and soaring mountain ranges, and the quiet elegance of a rose petal.

We enjoy the symphonies of nature too: the spring call of the meadowlark, the lyrical notes of a mountain stream tumbling over a waterfall, the whoosh of the wind whipping through the pines, and the sound of the surf crashing on a rocky shore.

We can start to experience Earth as my Guide experienced her home, Heaven.

Remember that the natural world is a tremendous gift. It sustains and nourishes us. We're utterly dependent on it for our survival. We have no other place within our solar system that we can call *home*. When we *feel* gratitude for this gift we send a message of love and appreciation back to the universe and Spirit for what we've been given.

We have but one world, and just one chance to love, cherish, and enjoy it as the people we are now. More importantly, our children and grandchildren will have only one chance as well — what legacy do we want to leave for them? Our actions today can have a profound effect on those who will come after us.

My Thoughts

In the midst of my NDE, I felt the depth of love that God has for all of nature, including our Earth. That spiritual love flowed through everything.

All of nature, this Earth, is a miraculous creation no matter what origin story you hold dear. Whether you follow the teachings of science, a religion, or something in between, this planet we call home is a pretty miraculous place. Even if there are other habitable planets in our galaxy or universe, our small planet is, for now, the only one on which we can survive. It is our home in the universe, the one place that we know of that truly allows for life as we know it to flourish. Think about that for a moment. We have no other place for billions of miles in any direction that could nourish our lives. Where would we be without air to breathe, water to drink, and food to eat?

Spiritually speaking, the energy of creation, of love, is in every atom of every galaxy, solar system, and planet. It infuses everyone and everything on our own Earth, too.

I could see and feel loving, spiritual energy through everything when I was in Heaven. As I walked through the Heaven's forests with my Guide, I could see the energy of love and life humming everywhere around me. The sky shimmered with it. The breezes moved in response to love. Spiritual love bloomed in every flower, and grew in every blade of grass.

Spirit and Earth and the universe all exist together. This concept became clear to me in Heaven, special in a way that is hard to put into words. My Guide allowed me to experience it by showing me how everything was connected. I saw the connections as if they were strands of a spider's web made of pure energy. An infinite number of gleaming, translucent strands ran through all I saw and sensed. This web also connected everything between the spiritual and physical realms – I somehow *felt* that truth at the center of my soul.

What happened when I came back to Earth? I still sensed this loving presence through everything here, too. I stopped seeing Earth as simply a playground and instead saw it as belonging to something much bigger than me; a miraculous gift that is available to experience, but in the end, not really *belonging* to anyone. You and I have this place to experience as fully as we can, to enjoy life in all its nuances and revel in it, but when our lives end the Earth passes along to others. The next generation of people will come along and live with what we've left them. So too will the next generations of animals and plants. In time, oceans will change shape, new mountain ranges will appear while the ones we know now will erode and soften, and rivers will cut new canyons. But that is for generations far into the future to witness.

All of us who are here, now, are simply caretakers of this amazing place.

During my physical recovery, I took short walks and on those walks I sensed that every atom here seemed to be infused with some kind of miraculous energy, too. Once I could make sense of what I was experiencing, everything in the world around me took on an aura of sacredness:

- The dandelion pushing its way through the cracks in a city sidewalk in order to send up its cheerful, yellow blossom.
- The mountains' snowmelt that gives rise to a gurgling little creek — the one that is home to trout, kingfishers, midges, and dragonflies, and where our small town gets its drinking water.
- The bright blooms of the daisies and marigolds in my deck planters are special, as are the waves of wildflowers blooming in the high alpine meadows.

All are spiritual miracles at the deepest level.

My Guide expressed that she would like more of us to treat the Earth and nature as such.

Connections

Modern science is demonstrating the interconnectedness of Earth's ecosystems. An event that happens in one place can greatly impact another part of the Earth. A simple example is: heavy downpours of rain over a large area can cause a river to flood, inundating farms and wetlands for hundreds of miles downstream. That same overflow of water can bring valuable minerals and nutrients to the wetlands where the river meets the sea, enriching plant life and feeding the animals.

We are also intimately connected with all of nature. It gives us life. We are dependent on nature for our survival. To mistreat it is, in the end, to mistreat ourselves. If we pollute a waterway with untreated waste from our chemical plants, where does that pollution go? It eventually gets back into us through the very water we drink and the food we eat.

But it also runs much deeper than that. During my time in Heaven, I was given the full force of the feelings of sadness my Guide has about how we treat our home planet. When she allowed me to feel her disappointment, I couldn't tolerate its intensity and collapsed onto my knees into the grass.

From our actions as a species, we don't seem to appreciate what we have here, let alone feel reverence for it.

She explained her view: nature is precious. The fact that we don't see this, and that we take it for granted or take advantage of it really bothers her. The sunrise over an open prairie filled with flowers, wildlife, and native grasses serves us and Spirit by just being beautiful. To do things that consistently destroy this beauty is disrespectful and not loving of Earth and our own spiritual connections.

She also saw that we are effectively shooting ourselves in the foot by not taking better care of our home. It was both funny and sad at the same time — she actually showed me a vision of a human shooting himself in the foot when she taught me about taking care of our Earth. As I've said before, we are intimately connected with our environment — the raindrops that fall on our garden may one day be part of the first tears of a newborn.

Most importantly, this world, this universe, and all that is in it does not really belong to us. It's here to nurture and sustain us, but in the end it's not ours. How could we treat this beautiful creation with disrespect? How could we go to religious services on the weekend and then, in good conscience, send a barge of trash out to sea to be dumped in the ocean on Monday?

My Guide thinks we can do better, and so do I.

Does this mean we're not supposed to live, eat, and breathe?

No. But it does mean that we do the best we can to protect what we have and use it wisely. We can aim to have as little negative impact as possible on our immediate environment and the planet. It also means that we try to make things better when and where we can, to the best of our abilities.

None of us is a superhero, but if we each do what we can, it will add up to something big.

One of the things that occurred to me later is that some of us *have* taken steps to make changes. By eliminating the use of DDT in the USA, for example, we've saved many species of birds from extinction. Remember the bald eagle, osprey, and falcons? We changed policy and in the process saved entire ecosystems. We *are* capable.

We can learn how to truly live with respect and in harmony with our planet. We can learn to be deeply grateful for what we've been given. We are capable of caring for our Earth while still continuing to live the gift of life that we have.

This will mean that as a planet, as nations, and as individuals, we might have some tough choices to make. I certainly don't have the answers, but *we* do, together.

First: love, respect, and gratitude. We seldom destroy what we truly love and cherish, so our first task is to learn to love, respect, and be truly grateful for the gift we have in this planet.

While the sights and feelings of Heaven were amazing, what we have here on Earth is no less wonderful. Whales sing in our beautiful oceans, mountains soar taller and grander than any skyscraper, beautiful beaches beckon us to relax, and prairies where the sky seems to go on forever show us humility. I bet you can think of at least three very places very special to you.

My Personal Ethic

Nature has always been my home and refuge. I see it as an entity in its own right, deserving of respect and love just as we humans are. Without its lifegiving water, oxygen, and soils, we wouldn't be here. We cannot survive without the natural world, plain and simple.

My personal ethic has been to love and respect the Earth and all of its inhabitants. But since coming close to losing my own life, and experiencing some form of instant "enlightenment," I seem to be developing something deeper — a profound sense of reverence.

Reverence means to have deep respect, awe, and even veneration for something. When I say I revere the Earth, what does that mean in my own life? My *needs* are getting simpler and less materialistic all of the time. I still use paper, drive a car, and take vacations, but I try to minimize my consumption. I also harbor a deep feeling of gratitude for what we have here on this small planet, for the gift we've been given in this Earth. It really is our small life raft in a universe of strange places.

I try to minimize my impact by using less, buying fewer "toys," being OK with an older car, recycling, encouraging organic farming by purchasing local and organically grown food, and donating time and money to conservation organizations. I also feel driven to write about nature and, through my writing and speaking, help others see the beauty and spirit in this beautiful place we all call *home*.

In the words of my Guide:

"While your life's time on Earth is relatively short, its impact may be felt for many of your generations.
Get out and enjoy the gifts of Nature that you have been given. Flowers in a pot on a balcony can be a reason for you to pause in your busy day and reflect on the concept of beauty. The sounds of birdsong may help you de-stress from a long, difficult day at work. A walk through the park with your children can help you reconnect with them and what it was like to be young.
Learn to stare in wonder at the beauty of a tree. Contemplate the colors of autumn leaves skittering across the lawn in the wind. Allow the serenity of a deer feeding its newly-born fawn to transport you to a peaceful place in your mind and heart."

PRACTICE REVERENCE

One very important thing you can do right now, and it won't cost you a thing, is to try to look at the world around you with a new perspective. This is what I did spontaneously when I re-entered the world. See all of nature as spiritual love taking physical form. The mountains, the beach, the rivers, the prairies, the deserts are all the love of the Divine made physical. Take a walk and try to look at nature in that light.

CHAPTER 9

We Are Creative and Powerful

EACH ONE OF US IS **more creative and powerful than we can possibly imagine. We have almost unlimited power to love, create, live in harmony, and to live in a spiritual way.**

FULL MESSAGE

In Heaven, I was allowed the gift of seeing into the heart of everyone and everything. Walking through the landscape with my Guide almost overloaded my mental and spiritual capacity with images, feelings, and knowledge. I could see many layers of *beingness* and power below the surface of everything. I could see the light of Spirit at the heart of my Guide, and I could sense her power and creativity. And I understood that everyone on Earth has similar power and creativity inside.

As we walked into a flower-filled meadow, ablaze with indescribable colors and loving energy, my Guide showed me just how powerful and creative I was. She gestured for me to touch a tall, daisy-like flower. As with everything else in heaven, Divine energy pulsed within it. But as I touched the flower, a level of emotional colors burst forth under its surface. The colors changed in response to emotion.

It seemed they were the color equivalent of the vibrational energy of a particular feeling. And I was the source.

That's when she then explained that the landscape I saw around me was, in part, driven by me. My own being connected with the energy of Divine love to create the landscape around me. I was, in part, the source of what I was experiencing.

Then our talk turned to Earth.

Every person on Earth has amazing power and creativity. At our cores we are shining beings of light, love, and energy who are living as humans in this time and place. Inside each one of us is a spiritual spark, a light-filled being capable of almost anything.

In the New Testament, Jesus spoke to this fact several times. Two passages I enjoy reading are in Matthew 17 when He healed a child after his followers had failed, and in John 14.

Speaking to the crowd, Jesus told them of the power within each one of us:

> *"He [Jesus] replied, "Because you have so little faith. Truly I tell you, if you have faith as small as a mustard seed, you can say to this mountain, 'Move from here to there,' and it will move. Nothing will be impossible for you."*
> *~Matthew 17:20 (NIV)*

And:

> *"Very truly I tell you, whoever believes in me will do the works I have been doing, and they will do even greater things than these…"*
> *~John 14:12*

Does this mean that each one of us can go out and heal ill family members at this moment?

Probably not, because we've been enculturated to believe it's not possible. But it does hint at the very powerful, bright spark that is hidden at our cores.

Jesus was a very special, spiritual being. He walked every day in clear connection with God. That connection to Spirit, as well as his own innate creative abilities, are something we can aspire to emulate even if it's in small amounts.

We each have individual, creative gifts that allow us to fully express ourselves, our love, and our connection to Divinity. Each one of us can tap this creative energy as long as we know in our hearts that we can. We have access to an infinite well of loving, creative energy, but many of us don't know about it or choose to ignore it. It is there, waiting for us.

By accessing it, by expressing this inspired creativity, we are again displaying our love and gratitude for the gifts we were given.

This doesn't mean that our creative gifts must be artistic like being a painter, musician, or sculptor. We have many avenues available to us to tap into this well of creativity. Perhaps you are a master at restoring old cars or homes; maybe you bake and decorate beautiful cakes; perhaps you are an inspired grade school teacher, floral designer, storyteller, or house painter. Or maybe your creativity lies in solving mathematical problems, engineering a new type of solar panel, or designing sports cars. Your creative power might be in raising loving, healthy children who will go on to be great gifts to all who know them.

Anything you do has the potential to draw on this well of inspiration and creativity, the well that goes beyond your own being and taps into something bigger and grander than us as humans.

Even living in a thoughtful, mindful way is being creative.

Live your gifts as fully as you can. Express them. Enjoy them. Have fun with them. Your talents may not necessarily lead you to an exciting new job, but they may allow you to connect with yourself, others, and Spirit in new and unique ways.

For example, a budding young novelist may follow her calling and join a writer's group where she meets her future husband. A knitter may seek out a knitting class and make a deep friendship with another participant that will last the rest of their lives. A young college student may decide to change his major from engineering to medicine and make a grand discovery that helps thousands to heal.

Express your talents, inspiration, and creativity with joy and follow them to where they may lead you. Don't fear these gifts. They are a powerful part of you.

Powerfully In-Spirit

Using our creativity, we have the power to bring something into existence. A painting, a piece of music, a beautiful building, an idea that brings peace, even a baby's new life starts with a spark of creativity or imagination. The power that we have to create is immense. We should not take it or ourselves lightly, although we often do.

We each are amazing and powerful people buried there behind our fears and insecurities. Our real power doesn't come from ruling countries or controlling everyone around us. It comes from our own creative sparks, our thoughts, what is in our hearts, the decisions we make, and the interactions we have with other people. When all of these factors work together in harmony and love, we can accomplish almost anything that feels right or good.

My Guide called this *living in-spirit*. When we live this way more often than not, it means we are living in alignment with our true selves.

Living in-spirit is ultimately a life choice we make, but we do need to practice it, and remember to have fun too. It's not easy and we'll never be perfect. After all, we're human.

"Unlearning" is a part of the practice. Often unintentionally, our families, teachers, and society can instill in us the idea that we are limited and lacking in our abilities. It takes a bit of work and practice to let go of this confining thinking and develop our own sense of self and wisdom. But believing in our abilities, and then living bigger, more fulfilling lives, does get easier over time.[18]

Start by questioning some of the things you've simply assumed to be true or necessary in your life. Where did that assumption come from? Does it serve you? Does it feel right to you? Is it rational or logical? For example, you might have been taught as a child that you're not creative, or that pursuing a creative endeavor is a waste of time. Where did you learn this? Perhaps your parents taught you this, or friends, a teacher, or another mentor. Does this assumption serve you now? Can you let it go and be more open-hearted with yourself? Is there some creative outlet you'd like to explore?

Living In-Spirit

What did my Guide mean by living in-spirit? It means making decisions and taking actions that allow us to follow the "map" that we have in our hearts. Any action or decision that brings you closer to living a positive life in love and joy is in-spirit. Deciding to perform your music for your church or community and doing it to the best of your abilities can be an in-spirit activity if it is done with love and positive intention. Taking the time to help your child who is struggling with his homework can be living in-spirit if you have love in your heart while helping him.

So too is being you, fully and unabashedly, as long as you are not impinging on someone else's joy and happiness. Living life as the best *you* that you can be and allowing your own internal light to shine brightly through your personality, talents, health, well-being, and joy in being alive is living in-spirit.

Taking care of your body and mind so that you can let your light shine fully is also living in-spirit. Eating in a healthful way, getting

---

18 If you're having a lot of difficulty in your life and feel that things are spiraling out of control, I strongly suggest you seek guidance from a religious leader, chaplain, counselor, or therapist. You're not alone, and help is available.

exercise, drinking clean water, and avoiding addictions all strengthen that connection to your source.

If going outside to watch the sunset makes you feel connected to life and love, then do it. Take your kids and make an event of it! Teach them different ways that they too can live in-spirit. What a blessing you could be to the little ones if you simply teach them this one concept: that living in love and light is a choice we all make.

At the end of the day, look back and contemplate, "if this were my last day on Earth, would I be happy with the person I was today? If not, what can I do differently tomorrow so that I am happy with who I am?"

THOUGHTS, WORDS, ACTIONS, AND MANIFESTING
A related idea, popular in New Thought culture, is the concept of "manifesting" or actively working to bring things into our lives. This concept has been around in various forms for a long time even though it's only become part of popular culture in the last decade or so.

The concept is simple and not really steeped in magic: through a combination of our thoughts, words, feelings, and actions, we can actively bring things into our lives or shape our experiences. Again, this isn't magic, nor is it rocket science. It's also subject to the whims of fate and events in life that we can't predict.

The bonus is that living actively in-spirit as much as possible amps up our abilities to bring positive experiences, people, and even things into our lives.

How? I'll leave this as a cliffhanger until Chapter 15.

MY THOUGHTS

As a longtime visual artist, being creative has been second nature to me for most of my life. New ideas for paintings come to me constantly. So many, in fact, that I have to pick and choose which ones to bring into existence. I can't possibly create fast enough to give life to all of the paintings that come to me.

I love this aspect of being a visual artist: having an idea seem to appear out of nowhere, then being able to make it take shape on canvas with paint and brushes still seems almost a miracle to me. I've worked hard for many years, taken classes and workshops, and destroyed a lot of failed paintings, but the process still feels sacred, almost magical. I feel blessed to have this ability and enjoy using it as much as possible.

In my scientific and technical life, creative problem-solving was second nature, too. It still is. I don't know that anyone ever taught this to me. It seems I always understood that if I am faced with a problem, I need to gather up information about it and allow my mind and soul space and time to work on the solution. Eventually, a solution will come. I know it will. And it does.

It's just natural for me.

I've hung out with creative folks most of my life, so it might not surprise you to learn that I have a hard time understanding how so many people simply refuse to see or acknowledge the vast amount of creativity and creative power inside of them. Everyone is creative in some way, *everyone*. Your creative abilities won't be anything like mine, and mine won't be like my friends', but each person is creative in some capacity.

When a non-artist finds out I'm a painter, I usually hear something negative about his or her own abilities:

- "I can't even draw a straight line." (Me: neither can I, not without a ruler.)
- "I could never come up with ideas like that." (Me: yours might be even more imaginative.)
- "I'm not the least bit creative." (Me: yes, you are, just in a different way.)

It's the last one that bothers me the most, especially now, after my time touching the realm of Spirit. I can see that creative spark inside each person, now. It's there in everyone. Whether we realize it or not, negative self-talk like this truly does cause our minds to believe that we are limited and that we can't do *it* (whatever "it" is). If we don't think we can do it, we probably won't even try.

I think that's called a self-fulfilling prophecy.

Seems that most of us would prefer to believe in and live lives of limitation than to explore and push the boundaries of what we actually can do.

We are all creative and we all have the capacity to exhibit that in different ways. Creativity is our birthright. It's not something gifted only to a few; it's in all of us. Your creativity might be preparing exquisite meals for guests or planning out memorable weddings. Maybe you're a physician and have an uncanny ability to diagnose and successfully treat rare diseases. Or you might be a teacher with great abilities to instruct learning-disabled students in math concepts.

These are only a few ways that we can experience and express our creativity. Our powerful and creative selves aren't reflected only in our jobs or hobbies, they come out in our interactions with others.

We can use care-filled, positive words and actions to bring peace and love to those around us. Just think about a gifted psychologist who treats veterans with horrible cases of Post-Traumatic Stress Disorder (PTSD). She uses her knowledge and creative power every day to help heal others' shattered lives. As another example, our own words can also offer comfort to a friend who's grieving a recent loss. Just think about that for a moment; our creativity and talent can make a profound difference in the lives of others.

Alternatively, if we're not conscious of what we're doing, we can create turmoil by using negative words and acting in thoughtless, cruel ways by destroying rather than creating.

This is one way we create our own reality, and it's how we use our powerful influence to impact the lives of others.

Healing

Can we perform miracles as is claimed about Jesus or other spiritual masters?

I believe it's possible for some enlightened beings, and my Guide showed me images of people like you and me bringing healing energy into the lives of others. She showed me images of people healing others with a touch, or with prayer, or belief. While I believe her at a spiritual level, I haven't seen that kind of healing for myself here on Earth. I *have* seen that we can help heal others through the words we speak and the actions we take, though.

Think about it. Acting with love and kindness toward others feels good for both us and the recipient. Speaking words of compassion and acting kindly to others may help them heal their own woundedness. I'm not sure if I will ever be able to heal my friends or family through the laying on of hands or through prayer, but I can act and speak in loving and compassionate ways to try to bring some healing to others in my life.

And I do know that I can help heal myself.

The healing power of my own body awes me. Bones that the SUV shattered are now fully healed or healing on their own with no conscious thought from me. I can and do control what I eat, how I think, my activity level, and the amount of stress in my life, but I don't consciously direct the knitting of my bones. It happens on its own. I can support that healing, though, through nutrition, exercise, and maintaining a healthy, positive mind. The same is true with my still-healing brain. I can feed it correctly, exercise it properly, and get the right amount of rest, but I can't consciously direct how the neurons grow back in a detailed way. My body and brain take care of that for me, and very efficiently too. My part of the equation is to support that healing brain nutritionally, and exercise it with techniques taught to me by my neurologist.[19]

---

[19] Mental exercises, painting, physical activity, getting adequate sleep, and meditation have helped my healing brain immensely.

The gift that I have in this body is utterly incredible.

Part of my healing includes spending time in contemplation every day. Meditation, mindfulness, ceremonies, prayer, and contemplation have been shown to reduce stress and ease anxiety and depression. New evidence suggests that they might be able to heal more physical ailments as well.

The well-documented "placebo effect" gives us a hint of the power of the mind to heal the body or improve symptoms of disease. And new research by physicians is starting to uncover the abilities that we have to heal ourselves[20]. Spontaneous healing is a powerful but little-studied phenomenon in which people with serious diagnoses experience complete healing or reversal of disease.

Those who experience spontaneous healings have some things in common, such as:

- Taking it upon themselves to make positive and drastic changes in their lives. This might include ending toxic relationships or changing jobs to something more in line with their personalities.
- Putting themselves and their health first by making positive changes to eating and exercise habits.
- Learning to practice gratitude.
- Developing their spirituality.
- Finding ways to reduce stress, such as taking up meditation, contemplative prayer, or biofeedback.

If you're faced with a situation where you need to heal, I recommend you seek out appropriate medical care and also research some of the books and papers written on spontaneous healing. Also consider your current lifestyle and its stressors, and what you can do to decrease or eliminate them.

---

20 See the work of Drs. James Nicolai, Andrew Weil, or Jeffrey Rediger for more information.

PRACTICE CREATIVITY

Below are just a few things I teach my students to encourage them to fan the flames of creativity in their lives. These have worked for me. Maybe one or two of them will work for you:

- *Find and acknowledge your creative passions.* What things did you love as a child — do you still carry that love forward? Is there a latent talent you have that you'd like to develop further? Is there some creative pursuit you always wanted to try but were afraid to start? Brainstorm things that you have a knack for, interest in, or wanted to try. Write them down, then go over the list to see if one or more resonates with you.
- *Commit yourself to developing one of your interests or talents.* Take classes, study books, or find a mentor to help you develop your talent or interest. Many community colleges, community centers, or even craft stores offer low-cost classes the area you would like to study.[21]
- *Take a little time out of your day for quiet contemplation, meditation, prayer or a contemplative walk.* In my own experience, my creativity is enhanced by spending quiet time alone, letting my thoughts wander, and allowing things to come into my mind at random. For me, a combination of quiet time coupled with allowing my mind to wander holds a key to unlocking more creativity.
- *Pay attention to dreams and the thoughts that come into your mind when you're sleepy.* Some of my most innovative painting ideas have come to me as I'm waking up in the morning.
- *Join a club or group in your area of interest.* For example, writer's groups are pretty easy to find and can be extremely valuable sources of creative inspiration.

---

[21] I teach a class and workshop called "Your Creative Voice: Finding and Nurturing Your Muse." For more information, see my website, NancyRynes.com .

CHAPTER 10

We Are All Connected

―⦅⦆―

EACH ONE OF US, ALL of us, and all of creation, are connected to, and through, Spirit.

FULL MESSAGE

When I woke up in the recovery room after my surgery and near-death experience, I reeled at the wrenching feeling of loss, of being torn away from Heaven and that palpable connection to Spirit. In Heaven, I had reveled in the feeling of deep connection to everyone and everything. I could feel the Divine and His love flowing through me. Through that Divine connection, I felt tendrils of contact with other beings, including my Guide. I felt part of a larger, loving whole, while at the same time I felt my own *beingness*. I was part of a massive network of love and light that buoyed me up and gave me the warmth of a thousand suns inside.

But coming back here, that feeling of connection felt dimmer almost immediately, and it's the one thing I've struggled with the most in the year or more since my experience.

How often have we heard about the concept of "oneness" or interconnectedness of all things? It sounds kind of hippie, doesn't it? We might talk about it within the confines of our religious institutions, and popular spiritual literature today discusses this topic often, yet how many of us actually believe it, practice it, or view life this way?

In Heaven, I learned that as I looked into the eyes of another human, I was gazing on a part of God. That's one way we can experience Divine connection here on Earth. That Divine presence is a part of the person across the aisle from us when we're on a plane or bus. Spiritual love lives in her heart. Spirit's joy suffuses his soul. And that person you are looking upon is special too, just as you are.

It is hard for us on Earth to hear or see that spiritual spark inside of others because of our busy-ness, our distractions, and the noise of life. We struggle to notice that someone who annoys or angers us also has a spiritual center, a core of Spirit's presence, just as we ourselves do. But try to remember that in a very real way, we are all connected to each other through our ties to Spirit.

At our cores, people are pretty much the same across the world. We have differences on the surface, such as skin color, political leanings, or culture, but below all of that we're more similar than different. We want to love and be loved. We want to raise our kids to have better lives than we had. We feel compassion for others who are hurt or struggling. We want to help those who need help. We feel pain and grieve during times of loss, and revel in joy at the births of our children. And most of us follow some kind of spiritual or philosophical path that often emphasizes love, compassion, and service to others.

Deep down where it counts, we're connected by these core needs, desires, beliefs, and drivers.

We're also connected to each other through the physical nature of being human. We need water, food, shelter, air, and clothing to survive. We share one small planet, Earth, that gives us, the plants, and the animals life. Because we share this planet and use its resources, we are connected intimately with all of nature. The water we drink can easily be polluted by an accident at one of our chemical plants, or the food we grow easily devastated by a flood. Life on Earth is like the web of a spider — touch one strand and the rest reverberate in unison.

> *"Humankind has not woven the web of life.*
> *We are but one thread within it.*
> *Whatever we do to the web, we do to ourselves.*
> *All things are bound together.*
> *All things connect."*
> ~Chief Seattle, 1854

Besides what my Guide relayed to me, in a way that's probably impossible to fully explain, I *felt* this interconnectedness dancing through the landscape of Heaven: from tree to tree, among the hills, through the air, and eventually through me. Similar to how electricity might move through transmission wires, the energy of the Divine flowed everywhere in the realm of Spirit.

Once I came back to my life, I realized that I could feel and sense the energy of *oneness* here too, although it was muted. I saw and felt it all around me in more subtle ways: in everyone who came to visit me during my recovery, in the hospital and medical staff, and eventually in the world outside. I began to sense the similarities and connections rather than the differences. I remembered reading about Native American spirituality and how some tribes revered the interconnectedness of life, but I never really *got it* before. Now I could actually experience it for myself every day. And often, seeing and experiencing this connection to the world around me causes me to be so overcome with joy that tears come to my eyes.

My Guide hoped that learning this concept of life's interconnectedness would allow us look at others and the world around us in a new way. She hoped that we might start to see the world as one big web of God's energy. Where can you find those connections to the Creator? Everywhere. All around you. Look. Be still. Listen. Most of all, listen within your own heart. That is where God sings joy for your life — right there inside of you.

Practice seeing Spirit all around you because everything, everyone, is ultimately connected through that spiritual energy. Everything is a part of that creation. Spirit is the ultimate inventor and artist! Every tree has a bit of the Creator inside, each person, every animal, every flower, the rocks, the Earth. All are connected to and through God.

My Thoughts

I still experience times when I find it difficult to feel my connectedness to others, but I am learning to see that God is in everyone, and through that spirituality we're all connected.

I've taken it as a personal goal to see that spiritual light in people I don't like or agree with. When I was in that near-death state, I learned that I will never *enjoy* everyone and don't need to be friends with everyone I meet, and this is OK. But I *could* see Spirit inside each person if I allowed myself to open my eyes and really look. I could also try to love each person at the most basic spiritual level, simply because of his or her connection to the Creator.

While it may be difficult, Heaven asks us to at least have a knowing that Spirit is there in everyone and in all we see in our world. Knowing that web of connection exists through all things might prompt us to try to treat ourselves and others with the love and respect that we all deserve.

One thing my Guide stressed, though, is that it's not OK to allow someone else to mistreat or abuse us, and it's not OK for us to mistreat or abuse others. We may know that Spirit's light resides in an abuser but we need to love *ourselves* enough to walk away from the person or the situation if we're being mistreated. Our spiritual source doesn't want us to be doormats!

Similarly, we have an obligation as adults to treat others with as much love and respect as we can muster, in every situation. We may get angry at our children for doing something we don't like, but this is not grounds for us to abuse them either physically or verbally. Words can damage just as much as physical violence does — it's simply more difficult to see on the surface.

Personally, I think this message of interconnectedness is a goal for a lifetime for me. While the message itself is relatively *simple*, it's certainly not *easy* to always look at others and see our mutual connection to God. Even harder is treating them with love and respect when they are not extending the same courtesy back to me.

But then I guess if it was easy, we would all be treating each other in this way automatically.

PRACTICE CONNECTION

Seeing the interconnectedness of life takes practice. From growing up on a farm, to spending many hours out in nature, and studying the natural sciences at university, I think I have a slightly easier time understanding how everything is connected in the natural world. I grew to adulthood witnessing the seasons of nature, seeing the cycles of birth, life, and death, and watching how animals and plants depend on each other.

More difficult for me is forging connections with other people and building a community of support around me. That still takes practice. It's not always comfortable, but I continue to push myself to grow a circle of friends and colleagues around me.

Each person will have a different method for seeing the connections in life. So too, each person will have different ways of forging new connections and building a community. Below are a few things that have helped me. Use them as a starting point but I encourage you to develop your own ways of connecting:

- *Work through the exercises at the end of Chapter 6: Love and Compassion.* These can help you see the divinity in yourself and others.
- *Contemplate the connections in nature.* Go to a stream, a lake, a forest, the mountains, or a seashore and notice the plants and animals around you. As an example, I might go to Mt. Evans outside of Denver and sit above tree line for a few hours. I notice that

the grasses and other plants are nourished by the water that fell as snow over the winter. They're fed by the decomposing granite beneath them. Animals like deer, mountain goats, bighorn sheep, pika, and marmots eat those grasses and plants in order to birth and raise the next generation of their kind. In a way, the animals are made of the stuff of that mountain, of the snow and rain that grace its slopes, of the minerals from the rock itself. Mountain lions, fox, and bobcats hunt the smaller animals on the mountain and so are also part of the web.

- *Think about the food you eat at supper tonight.* What are you eating? Do you know where it was grown? How did it get from the farm to your plate? It might be fun and informative for you to do an internet search on, "Where does my food come from?" You might be surprised to find that a farmer in southern California grew the lettuce in your salad; farm workers harvested it, then put it on a truck to take to a packaging center; the packaging center put the lettuce into crates; then a truck driver picked up the crates and brought them to a distribution center; from the distribution center, another driver picked up several crates of lettuce and brought them to your local supermarket. It's amazing the journeys our food takes and the number of people who help us eat every day.
- *You can do the above exercise with everything in your life:* your car, your home, your clothing, and your electronics.
- *Watch nature films on television, rent nature videos, or go to a natural history museum.* The best of these excel in highlighting the interconnectedness of natural ecosystems.
- *Find ways you can connect with others based on your own interests.* Join a club or a meetup group. Get involved in your local church or a political party. Volunteer to build trails through a nature area, or work with disadvantaged children.

CHAPTER 11

Allow, Let Go

A<small>LLOW</small> S<small>PIRIT</small> <small>TO</small> <small>WORK</small> <small>IN</small> your life. Let go of the need to control every little thing. Allow room for God to work in your life and see what amazing insights and experiences come your way.

F<small>ULL</small> M<small>ESSAGE</small>

Early in my tour of Heaven, while my Guide and I lingered on that first hillside overlooking the distant mountains, she gave me something very precious. She gave me a glimpse into what Spirit and Heaven felt like to her. Looking into my eyes, she somehow shared her mind and soul with me. For a few moments, I felt what it was like to be a spiritual being.

As I melded with her, my mind seemed to expand beyond anything I can describe. I felt deep connection with many other spiritual beings, and I could see those connections at an energy level: little gossamer threads of loving energy, of connection, coming in to me from many unseen souls.

I felt the deep connection to Divine love, and the constant communication with Spirit that permeated Heaven. And I experienced something else, something that startled me. I felt my Guide's *allowing* of Spirit to take care of everything. She didn't fight the flow of love and wisdom coming from the Divine. She simply relaxed spiritually and allowed Divine energy to flow into her and to work through her.

My Guide, and the beings who communicated through her, allowed the Divine to flow through them, to be a part of them, peacefully and fully. They didn't struggle, they simply *allowed*.

Once I had experienced this for myself, she severed that deep connection and allowed me to be myself again. I wouldn't have believed it if she hadn't shown me that glimpse.

Maybe because I wasn't fully in Heaven, or maybe because I was still tied to my human body which liked to control as much as I could around me, that concept of *allowing* seemed odd at first. My Guide simply trusted in Divine presence and didn't try to fight it. At times during my NDE, I was able to let go and allow, but it didn't feel natural for me. I struggled, most obviously when I was told that I'd be going back to my life.

That level of allowing I experienced in Heaven seemed more than I was capable of. But at the same time, I witnessed firsthand how powerful and freeing it was for my Guide to surrender to that loving presence. She didn't struggle; she simply allowed Spirit to work through her.

Have you ever had the feeling that a part of your life was an uphill battle, that no matter how hard you tried, something wasn't going the way you planned? Roadblocks and obstacles kept popping up out of nowhere. Things happened that seemed to derail you from the path you were on. Yet you stubbornly continued on in the direction you laid out for yourself, hoping against hope that eventually it would all work out.

Sometimes it does.

But other times that struggling only digs the hole deeper beneath your feet. Sometimes that struggling stands in the way of seeing a slightly different path that will allow you to get what you really need or want. More importantly, your struggles and stubbornness may get in the way of spiritual grace working in your life!

Let go. Give God room to do some of the work. You don't have to control everything.

Step back mentally and emotionally. Ask aloud for assistance and for guidance. Ask to have light shed on the situation, to make what is really going on, or what you should do, clear and obvious.

Have a dialog with Spirit. Let go, ask, and put your faith in that core of the Divine.

I learned that letting go and allowing Spirit to work in our lives is vitally important. In Heaven, this *allowing* is normal. Letting go is just a part of being connected to God.

But it's not so easy or natural here. For those of us on Earth, Spirit is simply asking us to let go of our tight-fisted control a little more.

If things aren't working the way you'd like in an area of your life, try something different. Let go of the need to control the minute aspects of that situation. Let go of your attachment to a specific outcome. Letting go a little might very well result in something even better coming into your life than you had expected!

Letting go of the need to control every little thing can also free up your mind so that it's open to insights, intuitions, or options that you couldn't see before. When you try to force a particular outcome, you may very well block your mind from other options and paths that could work better for you. So try not to control everything with a tight fist — let go a bit and see what other avenues present themselves.

Spirit does want us to continue to honor our commitments to the people we love or are responsible for, though. We still need to love and feed our kids and ourselves, support our families, and help our communities. But within those guidelines, we can learn to let go, even if it's a small amount.

Letting go of control of a situation, or even parts of a situation, isn't easy. It tends to scare us. We can't predict what might happen, so we try to control it even more. The reality is that there are very few outcomes we can predict. Anyone who's run a large project can tell you that unplanned issues crop up almost constantly and can derail the outcome if you're too tied to doing things a particular way. But a slight adjustment or course correction allows the team to complete the project on time and with better result that the original plan. In this case, letting go a little is a good thing. It opens us up to other possibilities.

What it ultimately comes down to is trust. Do we trust Spirit to show us the way? Do we trust ourselves: our intuition, heart, and mind?

Trying to control every little thing sends a signal that we really don't trust in the spiritual flow of life. Let go, ask for clarity. Then trust and listen. The Divine will make things clear if you take a mental step back and pay attention to your inner wisdom.

When the answer comes, be prepared to make a decision and to take action. For example, if you find out a business partner was not honest with you about something that really matters, perhaps you need to make some decisions about the relationship.

Continue to ignore spiritual guidance, though, and the connection to it will get progressively more muffled until one day you may not be able to hear it.

Spirit will be sad for this, although it will be allowed. This life is yours to live. You can live it with or without spiritual guidance. Ask for and accept that guidance and things will be a bit easier. Ignore that guidance and your whole life may feel like you are swimming upstream in a rushing river.

My Thoughts

I'll freely admit that *allowing* has not been one of my strong points in the past. As my Guide said, this is probably the single toughest thing we humans can face: letting go of the need to be in complete control of everything — every person, situation, event, and environment — and allowing a little room for Spirit to work.

The way my Guide put it to me is that in attempting to control everything, we effectively shut off our vision to many other good opportunities. We close the door to spiritual guidance with our need to control. Keeping the door open by letting go allows a little room for Spirit to work in our lives.

There is also another important point to consider. Spiritual guidance often makes itself known to us in our quiet moments: when we're praying, meditating, walking in nature, driving a car, sleeping, or other similar times. *If we allow ourselves to have more of these quiet, unstructured moments, we can better hear that guidance coming through our inner knowing, our hearts, and that "still, small voice" inside each of us.*

If you *must* structure your time, and most of us do to some extent, try to leave some quiet moments for yourself and God to commune. It might be that you choose to turn off your music during your commute, or schedule a 10-minute meditation in to your day. You might choose to take a quiet walk during a break at work or spend some time in prayer at the end of the day. Any one of these things, if done consistently, can open you to Divine guidance.

CONTROL

Most people have a strong need to control almost everything. We often try to plan our daily lives down to the second, not allowing for spontaneity, changes in schedule, or life events. We have homes with thick walls and windows to control our living environments and shut others out. Our yards are tightly manicured, lawns mowed to within millimeters of perfection, and hedges trimmed into unnatural shapes. We may try to control our kids and our partners or spouses, attempting to get them to do things our way, rather than allowing them to hear and follow their own inner wisdom. If we're in management positions at work, we often spend our days telling everyone who reports to us what to do. And while sometimes being a leader, mentor, or guide is appropriate, at other times, when we control *too much*, it can stifle those around us.

If something happens to upset our controlled life, it can throw us into a tailspin of fear, anxiety, and even more attempts to grasp control.

What I have learned through this process — both during my NDE and in the process of healing from my injuries — is just how little control we really *do* have over things in our lives. To borrow from Albert Einstein, control is an illusion, albeit a very persistent one.

If you think about it, the only things we can really control are our own thoughts, reactions, actions, and words. This is very important to understand. Take a minute to think about it.

You often can't control an outside event, like a hot water heater suddenly breaking, but you can control how you think about it, react to it, act afterwards, and the words you speak about it. If you allow your mind to continuously loop through how unfair it is that your hot water heater broke, you'll waste precious time and energy angsting about it rather than taking the needed steps just to fix it.

Fretting over the event itself, one that is done and you can't go back and change, doesn't solve anything. In fact, it creates more trauma or stress for you. You can choose something different. You can choose to think and act differently, which itself just might bring your solution into focus.

Engage your mind. Is there something positive you can take from the situation? Can you learn something as a result of what happened? If you need to make a course correction, maybe your new path will be better than the one you originally laid out for yourself. Think about ways that you can go forward in a positive direction.

Hold the past lightly. It's done and gone so try not to give it too much power in your life now. Spend your time and energy on fully seeing and experiencing the present moment, then think about a new way forward.

Holding on to what *was* instead of facing the reality of the present situation can also have negative consequences:

- Your mind and energy are stuck in the "should be" rather than facing the "what is" or even seeing the possibilities of what "could be."
- Your mind and energy are bound up in something that isn't working, which blocks you from hearing the guidance Spirit is sending your way.
- Your mind stays mired in anxiety and negative thoughts or emotions. Guess what? This doesn't feel very good!

Let It Go

So what should you do when a situation is spiraling out of control?

Well, if it's not life threatening or dangerous in any way (physically, mentally, and emotionally), ask for help. You can ask someone else for help, or you can ask for spiritual guidance from the Divine. People often are happy to help, and God is there to assist at all times, day or night. To ask God, stop what you're doing, take a few deep breaths, sit quietly, perhaps meditate or pray, and simply ask for help or guidance. I usually ask aloud, although others ask silently. You'll find which way works best for you. That's it. Seems pretty simple, doesn't it?

Oftentimes, the hardest part for me is waiting for the guidance to come. I'm sometimes not very patient, so of course I want answers *right now*. I've learned that Spirit can work on a different schedule than we do so I'm developing the fine art of waiting attentively for the guidance to come.

If you ask Spirit for clarity, it may come immediately or you may need to wait for light to be shed on the situation. If you allow yourself some quiet moments, it will be easier for Spirit to show you the way.

Sometimes I get a little bit forceful in my questions or requests for clarity if a situation is quickly spiraling out-of-control. I might ask, "God, what in the world is going on here? What do I need to see or do in this situation? Please make it clear and obvious to me as soon as possible."

Guess what? I usually get clarity very quickly, and usually so clearly that it's impossible to ignore.

You could also try to take a mental and emotional step back from the situation. If you can, let it rest for a while without giving it too much attention. This may not be possible, but try.

- Take some deep, belly breaths and physically walk away for a bit.
- Go for a walk or engage in some kind of exercise. Sometimes moving your body allows the mind to quiet and clarity to come.
- Get some physical distance. If the situation is severe, a trip to the beach or the mountains may help your mind settle down.
- Take some time in meditation, contemplation, or prayer.

- Think about the things that you *can* control surrounding the situation, take action on those things, then turn the rest over to Spirit.
- Ask about the situation, then contemplate possible avenues to take. You could do this aloud, or you might try writing. Write the question, then for several minutes, simply free-write whatever comes to mind. This can work better for some than contemplation.
- Say aloud or to yourself: "I let go of the need to have *xyz outcome.*" An example might be, "I let go of the *need* to win the salesman of the year award." Keep repeating that to yourself until it feels like you're really letting go (note: this approach doesn't work for everyone; it's simply one I use for myself).

At the very least, try to let go of the expectation, of the *needing* to have a certain outcome. Then simply take a mental and emotional step back and observe the situation from a higher perspective.

The *needing* to have a particular outcome can blind us to something better.

My Own Experience

Being hit by a truck, having a near-death experience, spending two weeks in the hospital, and the months of recovery that followed forced me to *really* deal with letting go in my own life.

There is nothing quite so eye-opening as coming that close to death. I know that I had done what I could to avoid the crash but in the end, the occurrence of the event itself wasn't up to me. Living wasn't fully up to me either. Medical professionals took over and saved my life, and my Guide sent me back to Earth even though my soul wanted to leave my body permanently.

Being returned to life while protesting strongly that I didn't want to go back solidified how little control I had over my path at that point. Arguing, throwing a temper tantrum, crying, and pleading didn't change the situation. I was still forced to return to living and fulfilling my commitments.

But I did have a choice as to how I lived my life. I could whine, complain, and continue to act like a toddler, or I could choose to go forward in a new way: strong, positive, upbeat, and excited to spread the insights and help people as much as I could. I chose the new, more empowered way.

While lying in the hospital, I realized I had *some* control over my healing process: in what foods I ate, in my attitude, in my activity level, in how I treated those around me, and in being my own advocate for receiving excellent care. I also came to understand there were some things I could *not* control: how nurses and doctors acted, the need for certain safety protocols, medical tests, procedures that would help heal me, and the abundance and transmission of germs in the hospital.

Instead of whining or being angry, I decided to focus on one tangible goal that I could influence: getting my body to the point of walking without assistance. I knew I had some control over that. I could positively impact my own healing process. And to save my energy, I let my concerns about everything else fade away for a while and leaned on the other people in my life for help and support. This allowed me to focus on that one goal of walking.

Realizing that I also controlled my words, I endeavored to speak to those around me in loving, grateful ways: my family and friends, the nurses, the nursing assistants, the doctors, the housekeepers, everyone I encountered. After all, they were a part of Spirit just as much as I was and deserved to be treated with respect and love, too.

The Near-Death Experience and Letting Go

Experiencing a near-death state often does change the way people look at life. How can it not? Facing death, seeing firsthand what might come at the end of life, and then returning to Earth changes people. It changed me in one important way: it's a bit easier for me to let go of control these days.

I'm no longer scared of or worried about death. Actually, I'm not scared of or worried about much of anything anymore! I guess because I've died and it wasn't all that bad, not much of this world frightens me. This one aspect of my experience has liberated me from the burden of the fears and worries I carried with me for most of my life. And it's those fears and worries that, I believe, drives us to want to control so much in our lives.

I now realize that much of this drama that we deal with as humans isn't really all that important on a grand, spiritual scale, and in reality, we create most of it for ourselves anyway. So then why the worry and the need to grasp desperately for control? Why not just let go and let Spirit work in my life?

A True Story about Letting Go

During my recovery, a friend commented on my upbeat attitude and positive outlook on life. He wondered how I could maintain it or even *if* I could maintain it. After all, he said, you deserve to feel victimized after what you went through these last couple of months. He wondered why I wasn't angry with the person who caused the injuries that almost left me paralyzed.

I'll admit that there was a time where wallowing in anger and self-pity is exactly what I would have been doing after an accident such as this one. But when I was 23, I met someone whose message forever changed how I looked at these tough events in our lives. While these events happened years before my NDE, I didn't internalize the wisdom I learned until after I came back from heaven.

During the summer of 1989, Andrews University and the Government of Jordan[22] hired me to be an archaeological artist on a dig just outside of Amman. My job was to draw each object found on the dig. This was no small task since the dig encompassed three distinct sites, the smallest being the size of an American football field, and the timespan of the dig ran back to about 3000 B.C.

---

22 Jordan is a small country in the Middle East, nestled between Israel and Iraq.

I had a lot of antiquities to draw, but I still found time to wander through Amman and soak up the culture.

On one of my forays into the city, I stopped at a small shop that sold ice cream and a bewildering array of confections. The owner of the store, a man of 55 or 60 years old, surprised me by striking up a conversation. Now this was very unusual for 1989 in Jordan. To have an older, married man start a conversation with a young, unmarried, unaccompanied foreign woman just wasn't done. But he explained that he had gone to university in the US and just wanted a chance to practice his English.

He stood about six feet tall and wore the typical jellabiya (long white linen robe) of the Middle Eastern deserts. His face was classic Arabic — beautiful aquiline nose, lean, sharp features, dark brown eyes, and very tan, weathered skin. His build was strong but lean, and he spoke flawless English. The artist in me wanted to paint his portrait.

During the course of the conversation, he let on that he was Palestinian.

Fear clutched at my belly. The late 1980s saw a lot of unrest between Palestinians and Israelis. During the few months I'd been here in Jordan, several innocent people had died in border skirmishes with Israel. The danger was real. I was here, alone, and no one at the dig knew exactly where I was. My first thought was: "I could be taken hostage. Dumb, dumb, dumb."

I think he saw the fear on my face and reassured me that I was safe. His smile and easy, relaxed demeanor allowed me to let my guard down a little.

I gathered my courage and asked him how he felt about the terrorism, the hatred felt between some of the Palestinians and the Israelis. I wanted to know how it had impacted him and his people, and if there was a way out of the circle of violence and anger.

He said that the violence greatly saddened him, that it was time to just let all of this anger and bitterness go and get on with the job of living in peace with each other. I asked if he really thought it was possible, to just let it go and move on with life.

He responded by telling me about himself: how in 1948, when he was a youngster still living with his parents just outside of Jerusalem, United Nations (U.N.) soldiers knocked on the door of his family's home one night. The U.N. forces were clearing out portions of what used to be Palestine to aid in the creation of the new country of Israel. He told me that the soldiers gave the family only a few hours to pack up their belongings, to leave the home they had lived in for many generations, and move.

They had no idea where they would go. They were now refugees.

In time, the family ended up in Amman where his father was able to start a small business. Eventually, the son studied in America and came home upon graduation to help with the business. This man in front of me said he had a good life: a beautiful wife and children, a business, a home, good health, but he admitted to missing the family home he knew and loved as a child. Although, he said, no family home was worth the violence gripping his people.

I asked him if he himself was angry or bitter, if he harbored any resentment towards Americans or the British. His answer moved me to tears and has stuck with me to this day.

No, he explained, while he missed his home, *what's done is done.* At first, he was angry about losing his family's home but he quickly realized that there was no point wallowing in negativity. Doing so would ruin the life that he was living now. He preferred to focus on the wonderful things he *did* have. He said that the U.N. forces were doing what they thought was right. And the Jewish people did deserve a home after what they'd been through. This man's only wish was that the U.N. and Israel would have given the Palestinians a chance to stay and live in peace with the new government. He believed it was possible, and still believed it was possible, but he understood the situation, too.

He said that *happiness was a choice, and so was living a life of hatred and bitterness.* His preference was to live a happy, peaceful life and get along with those around him.

What I realized was that he had wandered through a maze of anger and decided to come out into the light. Once he let go of anger and resentment, and made the choice of happiness, a beautiful life unfolded.

I remember this man every time I even start to feel bad about events in my life. He is right — what happens to us, happens. Often we have no control over it. But how we choose to go forward with our life is completely up to us. We can waste our time being angry or bitter, or we can let it go and embrace joy and happiness.

PRACTICE LETTING GO

It seems I've often struggled with the practice of giving up of the *need* to control everything in my life. Like so many, I felt the more I tried to bring things under my control, the better my life would be. Unfortunately, I've learned the hard way that's not always the case.

I understand that I need to practice letting go of the *need* to control everything. Below are a few things that have helped me with this:

- *Water exercise: Trying to control outside forces or other people is like trying to grasp water tightly in your hands.* Go to a sink and turn on the water. Cup your hands together under the stream of water and hold as much in your hands as you can. How do you hold your hands? Likely you will hold them cupped, pinkies together, with your hands open to gently collect as much water as possible. Now squeeze both hands into fists as if you were trying to grasp on to the water as tightly as possible. Go on, grab that water as hard as you can. Try to hold on to that water with all of your might! What happens? The water squirts all over and you completely lose the very thing you were trying to control. Life is often like this. The more you grasp at it, the more it evades you.

- *If you're having trouble letting go of something, ask for spiritual guidance in whatever way feels right for you.* It's OK to call on your spiritual source when you need help in letting go of something. Asking for help aloud usually works best for me.

* *Contemplate or meditate rising up above the situation, like a hawk.* From a more emotionally-distant vantage point, what do you see? What can you do differently? What don't you have control over? What can you control? What steps can you actually take that might positively influence the situation? Is there anything you can let go of and let Spirit handle?
* *Take action: is there something you actually can do to make the situation better?* Then do it.
* *Continue your focus on the things you can control and turn the rest over to Spirit (see the next bullet point for one way).* Then pay attention to your own internal guidance system, your inner voice, your inner wisdom, or your intuition to show you the next step to take.
* *The God Jar:* I learned this exercise several years ago. Get a big jar or vase that you don't use and clean it out. If you'd like to bless it with a prayer, go ahead, although this doesn't seem to be necessary. It is now your "God Jar." Prepare some small pieces of paper or index cards. They don't need to be big — a few inches square will do. When you have a worry or a situation you need help with, write about it on the paper. Now fold up the paper, put it in the "God Jar", and forget about it. It gets the problem off your mind and puts it on Spirit's list to handle.

Important note: If you are having thoughts of trying to harm yourself or someone else, are having recurring negative thoughts or nightmares, or truly can't let go of a situation, please seek professional help in the form of a psychologist, religious leader, chaplain, or trusted friend. You don't have to endure this alone — there is help out there for you.

CHAPTER 12

Allow Others to Show Love

*Show your love for others **by allowing them to show love. Allow them to help you when you need it. Allow them to be compassionate, to make their own decisions and choices, and to be responsible for their own lives. We are each on a different path. Love and respect the path each person is on, just as you would want them to love and respect yours.***

FULL MESSAGE

A part of our connection to others is the way that we come together to help each other. And just as we each have a desire to help others in need, others may want to help us when we need it. The kindest and most loving thing we can do is to let them. We can show our love or care to others by allowing them to show love, kindness, or compassion to us.

Many of us push others away when all they want is to lend a helping hand. Why? Pride, ego, the fear of being seen as "unable," maybe. In most situations, the best thing might simply be to let go and *allow*. It's OK to not be strong and in control of everything all the time. Allowing space for others to be strong, to lend a hand, and to shine their light is a most loving and compassionate gesture.

Helping each other starts the process of building a community around us, in Spirit.

Allow others to show love and support, even if it's in a small way. Leaving the space for others to be compassionate and giving, without ego or fear getting in the way, is a supreme act of love and trust. By opening up the space for others to help us, we aid them in living in the Light, to love as Jesus, Buddha, and St. Francis loved. How wonderful is that?

Yes, taking responsibility for ourselves and having a level of independence is important, but it's just as important to come together to build a community in Spirit. Allowing others to help us strengthens the bonds of our communities. If we look at what the word "community" means, we see:

Community:
Commun = shared
Unity = oneness, as one

Community = Shared as one; Coming together as one

Communities in the truest sense of the word are groupings of people with a common bond, coming together, and sharing *as one*. We might share a physical place, like a town, but we could also build a community around a shared goal or belief system. A community doesn't need to be a physical place — all it needs to flourish is a caring, sharing, like-minded group of people coming together for a common purpose. When we share with others by lending a hand, we build a network of support, of caring, and of love. In the most ideal communities, members enable each other to be their best. Allowing others to be giving and generous is one way to enable and encourage the best in each other and thus strengthen the community.

My Guide would like to inspire all of us to work more at building alliances of support, whether it's a community of friends, family, neighbors, church groups, or co-workers. She assured me that coming together in this way, in love and support of each other, would make a positive difference in everyone's lives.

Another thing she stressed is that in a healthy community, we allow other adults to follow their own path in life. This is a very delicate dance. It isn't our responsibility to try to dictate the life paths of other adults. We might assist in times of need, but the path another takes is ultimately up to him or her alone. Trying to control the path another takes in life disrespects him or her and undermines the true sense of community.

MY THOUGHTS

From the time I was a child, I had a fierce independent streak. I didn't want anyone to think I was unable, lazy, or weak so I turned down help constantly. I took pride in doing things for myself as much as possible — perhaps as a result of growing up on a small farm, or maybe I was simply trying to keep up with my older brothers. Whatever the reason, while I enjoyed helping others, I often didn't like other people trying to help me. Their offers made me uncomfortable somehow. I think a part of me felt as though I didn't deserve the attention or assistance, and I didn't want to owe anyone for the help they'd extended to me. I always wanted to fade into the background and I felt that people helping me drew too much attention. I didn't want the fuss or the spotlight.

What I didn't realize was that being so strongly independent actually pushed family, friends, acquaintances, and coworkers away — the same people with whom I wanted strong relationships.

I guess to others it might have looked like I didn't need or want anyone else and so people tended to drift away. That wasn't how I truly felt but I had no idea that it was my supremely independent streak that formed the wall between me and others. It didn't allow anyone to lend a hand, to come in to my life, or to be giving, caring, and compassionate. It was my form of protection, I guess. It safely kept most people at arm's length.

That worked pretty well, up until I was laid out in a hospital bed and completely dependent on everyone around me! Being effectively immobile for weeks made me realize just how little control I really had and how much I *needed* and *wanted* other people in my life. I also came to understand that it was OK to allow others to help me. Accepting help didn't mean I was weak or needy, it just meant I needed some help.

Letting go of that wall of independence seemed like a huge feat, but some advice from my friend Amy[23] made me stop and think. As I recovered from my injuries, my coworkers wanted desperately to help in any way they could. I didn't want to draw attention to myself and my condition, and I sure didn't want to trouble them in any way, so I resisted their offers. Amy came to visit me one day and laid it out in plain terms: my coworkers were in shock over what happened to me. They were good people but felt helpless and simply needed to do *something* for me. Anything. Helping me would make them feel better.

It was pretty tough to let go of that wall of independence until I realized how I might feel if the situation was reversed. Once I allowed others to give of their time or energy to lend me a hand, I saw that our relationships strengthened. People I had rarely spoken with at work offered to help with meals, move furniture, even run errands, no questions asked other than "What do you need?" The generosity of people I barely knew, as well as longtime friends and family, made me feel so grateful that tears often came to my eyes. And for the first time in my life, I understood what being a part of a strong community felt like.

Many of us have gotten away from that sense of community in our modern lives. We've isolated ourselves by choice or necessity. The electronic age can make it difficult to build true, in-person, meaningful friendships. We get caught up in online games, social media, and texting, forgetting that the real connection comes when we're face-to-face. I think we've also lost something else truly valuable and sacred: that sense

---

23 Amy Collette is my friend, editor, and also author of her own book called *The Gratitude Connection.*

of an almost tribal community that, in some ways, is so integral to being human.

For most of our time on Earth as a species, humans tended to live in small, close-knit communities or tribal groups. At the most basic level, these small groups helped us survive and thrive.[24] Today we live in large cities surrounded by millions of people, yet rarely speak to our neighbors and don't connect with co-workers any more than we have to. But that mental and emotional need to be part of a community is still ingrained in our psyches, perhaps even in our DNA.

Opening up some space in our independence, allowing others to help us, and in turn lending a hand to others is how we can start to form or strengthen a small community of support. I've seen this work within my own life. My trauma and recovery has been a blessing in a way. I've come to see the value in relaxing those defenses and letting others in. I understand now that I'm not a superwoman, I do need and want help sometimes. I've noticed that this softening of my walls of independence has helped me more easily build new relationships and strengthen existing friendships. Amazing what a little "allowing" can do!

The second part of this message deals with allowing others within our family or community, or even city or nation, to follow their own paths through life. We certainly wouldn't want someone else to tell us what religion to follow or whom we should marry, for example, yet we seem to think it's OK to expect others to take only the paths we approve of. This is a complex topic, and I'm not going to dive into it fully quite yet. But just let that sink in and I'll come back to it later in the book.

In any case, my Guide wanted to stress that allowing others to live their own truths and follow their own paths is part of living in a healthy family or community.

---

24 See the books of author Jared Diamond for more information on early human tribal life.

PRACTICE ALLOWING OTHERS TO HELP

Below are a few things I've done that have helped me make this message a part of my life. One or more of them might help you too:

- *Think about your life in the last few weeks. Has someone offered to lend a hand in a healthy, supportive, caring way?* Did you accept the help or not? If not, why not?
- *Think about some ways you might allow others to help you.* Then choose one and let it happen! Afterward, reflect on how it felt to allow someone to lend a hand.
- *Is there something you truly need some help with but are reluctant to ask for?* Perhaps you can gather up the courage to *ask* someone for assistance with a task. If you do ask, how does it feel? How does it feel to actually get the assistance you need or want?
- *Think about some ways you can help others. Can you assist an elderly neighbor to shovel her sidewalk clear of snow?* Do you have an ailing family member who needs to get to the grocery store or pharmacy? How about paying the fee for the person behind you at the toll booth or the entrance to the national park you're visiting? Think up a way to help another in the next week and just do it.

CHAPTER 13

Listen to Your Inner Wisdom

---

*LEARN TO LISTEN TO YOUR **inner wisdom**. **Follow its guidance. Your purpose and callings are here. Follow that small, quiet voice, for that is the true voice of Spirit in your life. When you have doubts, when you need guidance, your inner wisdom is there to lead you.***

FULL MESSAGE

During my tour of Heaven, my Guide stopped us in a small forest. We looked up at the light shining through the trees, marveled at its golden brilliance, and how it lit up the forest floor. That golden light shimmered with love and as it fell on me, I could feel it in my heart. That energy of light penetrated my skin and went right to the core of my being.

At that moment, my Guide gave me a vision of a giant map laid out all around me. It looked old, similar to one of those ancient nautical charts from the 1500s. The surface of the map appeared to be aged vellum. Lines drawn in ink indicated pathways. I saw little islands drawn that seemed to be at points where lines intersected. But alas, I didn't see any dragons at the edges.

It was the map of my life. Or rather, it was a map that showed me the many paths my life could take. My essence was superimposed over the center of the map and in my heart area, right where that light shone, she showed me the image of a compass. It was her way of saying that my heart or my inner wisdom is connected to the Divine (that light from above), and it's a compass that I can use to navigate the map of my life.

Wow. What a visual!

She explained that in Heaven, Divine guidance flows through all, constantly. It's always there to call on, and it's easy to hear and identify.

Even on Earth we have direct access to Divine guidance. It may not always be easy for us to access, but it is there if we know where to look. This guidance is what we call our inner wisdom, that internal sense of *just knowing*. It's what can help lead us in our choice of career, spouse, home, route home from work, or even vacation destination.

This inner wisdom might also tell us when a family member is hurting even though we're far apart. It can guide us in small decisions — whether to date someone or walk away, whether a place of worship is right for us, or whether that nagging pain in our side is something serious.

Our inner wisdom is a combination of our intuition or "gut-sense," our heart-voice, and our mind or learned knowledge. When accessed in concert, they can be powerful resources for us to call on when making decisions:

- Intuition is that sense of coming to a conclusion quickly, getting a flash of insight, or making a fast decision independent of long, thought-filled reasoning or logic.
- Our heart-voice is that emotional, feeling-sense that we might have when making a decision or meeting someone. It's our spiritual compass, a direct link to our spiritual source and spiritual wisdom.
- Our mind is a collection of our processed experiences combined with what we've learned either through formal channels, our families, or through life's hard knocks. The mind can be particularly susceptible to unfounded fears, pathologies, the effects of poor nutrition or health, or even "brainwashing" or propaganda.

As humans, it can sometimes be difficult to hear this combined voice of inner wisdom. In our physical bodies, living our daily lives, it can be hard to hear spiritual guidance through our hearts because our lives are filled with daily dramas, busyness, and activities. The voice of our heart is often quiet, sometimes just a whisper of a feeling. The same is true of our intuition. If we don't know *to* listen, or *how to* listen, we might just miss either one or both of them. The mind is a little louder, a little easier for us to access, but it can be prone to a host of problems and clutter that can cloud its message.

Have you ever wondered why the world's major religions incorporate some kind of prayer, meditation, or contemplation into their practices? In part, it's to quiet down the distractions of the mind so that we can better hear our intuitions and heart-voices.

My Guide showed me how prayer specifically can strengthen our spiritual connections. Those who pray often ask or even plead for some form of help. Those requests are welcomed, but my Guide suggested that we sometimes try "praying" by being quiet, by simply listening. Spirit welcomes this kind of prayer because it opens us to loving connection and guidance. Another way is simply to open up a verbal dialog with Spirit. Talk with God. Yes, really talk. Out loud. Remember, Spirit welcomes our conversation in good times and bad.

Even with practice, you still might not hear intuition or spiritual guidance over the chatter of your own mind. Practice stilling your mind too, in addition to your speech and hearing. Sometimes this quiet mind can happen spontaneously while you're doing something else: walking, sitting by a lake, riding on a train, or working on a craft. Have you had experiences where the world has seemed to fade away and all of your being is enraptured by the task at hand? What were you doing when this happened? Try recreating it. That is one way to practice the silence that you'll need in order to connect to that small voice inside your heart.

What will you experience when you connect to your inner wisdom? How will you know if Spirit is trying to communicate with you?

Sometimes it will simply feel like a flash of insight — perhaps knowing that you need to take a different route home from work, then later finding out your regular route had a two hour delay due to an auto accident. That's your intuition speaking. Or knowing that if you date a particular person, it will only lead to heartache. This may be your heart-voice, with your intuition and mind speaking too. Or just knowing, somehow, that it is OK to trust your new coworker. Intuition again, and your heart. Or that a decision you're making will be right because it simply *feels* right — heart-voice, and possibly intuition and mind too. If you listen to and acknowledge this type of inspired insight, it will likely become stronger and clearer over time. Try trusting it with something small and see what happens.

When I'm in doubt about a decision, I'll take some quiet time and do a three-part check and listen to what my intuition, heart-voice, and mind have to say. Are they in agreement? If not, why not? Am I feeling fear, and if so, what is its source?

But how do you choose if the voices don't agree? Ultimately, the way you proceed is up to you. For me, I am trying to lean away from making all of my decisions from my mind, so I will often err on the side of following my heart and intuition a bit more. That doesn't mean I ignore my mind, though. Instead, I listen to what it's telling me. Is there a warning I need to heed? Is there a potential pitfall I should watch for? I allow my mind to inform my decisions, but I don't necessarily cater to its every whim either.

It's fair to keep in mind that when doing the three-part check, any one of those sources of wisdom may be wrong or misguided. Our intuitions, hearts, and minds can and do make mistakes, although I find within myself that my mind is much more prone to errors than my heart or intuition are. How many times have you taken an instant dislike to someone you meet, but you later discover they are the kindest, gentlest, most compassionate person you know? It just happens that the day you met him, he was having a difficult morning and his mind was preoccupied with his troubles.

That's why it's helpful to check in with all three: intuition, heart, and mind.

Another thing to remember is that your heart-voice and your intuition might become confused by what's going on in your busy mind, too. If your mind is relatively clear, quiet, and calm, it's easier to feel and hear Spirit's tug through your heart and intuition. But if we're fearful, anxious, addicted, or otherwise emotionally or mentally challenged, this "static" can drown out those quiet yet Divinely-inspired voices.

Ignoring your inner wisdom can lead to heartache and troubles. Have you ever *known* a decision was wrong but you went ahead and did it anyway? Perhaps you later regretted it because that path led to disaster. Ignoring this inspired guidance can lead us away from our true selves, and ultimately away from our spiritual source. Ignoring this guidance may very well make its voice progressively quieter and harder to hear.

INNER QUIET

My Guide taught me that one of the most important things we can do for ourselves is to learn how to access our own inner wisdom. To make it easier, try to cultivate a quiet mind. We can begin to quiet our minds through prayer, meditation, contemplation, playing a musical instrument, going for a hike without any music or noisy cell phones, wandering through a meadow or forest, or even sitting and enjoying a place that is sacred or special in some way. If we remove ourselves from the distractions of modern life for a little bit each day, we can more easily learn to reconnect with our Divine Source.

FEARS

Many of us are bound up in fears, and fears will drown out our inner wisdom quicker and more thoroughly than anything else. Fear is the opposite of love. Fear is often not our friend, especially unfounded fear (i.e., fear without a concrete reason). For example, being fearful of someone who is intending to hurt us is justified and helpful, but being generally fearful without a direct reason or cause can harm us. This type of fear stresses our bodies and minds, causes anxiety, and makes that inner, spiritual guidance more difficult to observe.

Unfounded fear has many causes but can sometimes stem from a lack of trust: in God, in ourselves, a spouse, a boss, or others. We may also be susceptible to fears due to circumstances in childhood, things society taught us, television shows, the media, and many more. Learning to listen to and trust both our inner wisdom and Spirit can help us deal with our fears in a healthier way.

It might help you to ask yourself and your inner wisdom if there is truth in the fear. Is there something you can learn from it? Is there something you need to pay attention to? Does this situation or person remind you of something else that caused you hurt? Our subconscious minds can often see trouble where our conscious minds don't. The subconscious can alerts us to potential trouble though fear. For example, a woman who was abused as a child might feel an instant fear of a new acquaintance who happens to remind her of her abuser.

Think about the fear — is it trying to tell you something about a person or an event that your conscious mind can't see?

If the fear doesn't seem to have an apparent cause, sometimes thinking through it helps to dispel it. Mull over what could *really* happen in the situation that you fear, whether a dire result is truly likely, and what the other, more positive, results might be. Bring a little logic to the situation if you can.

Sometimes we just need to "feel the fear and do it anyway" (within reason of course, and when it's not going to harm us or someone else). Feel the fear. Think about it. Consider the risks involved. Then proceed on your path if the way ahead looks safe.

Unfounded fears can hinder us. They may make us choose the wrong careers, spouses, or friends. They will keep us from taking a leap of faith that will lead to a better life. They may make us choose the wrong road through life because it looks safer, even if it isn't a path that fully aligns with who we are.

Unfounded fear can often be overcome by going within, listening to your inner wisdom, considering the options and risks, listening to spiritual guidance, and trusting both divine wisdom and yourself to lead you to your right decision. And if you make a mistake, well, it might actually be a blessing in disguise.

My Thoughts

Five months after my accident, I made a pledge to live a year listening to, and following, the voices of my heart and intuition rather than blindly doing only what my brain told me I *should* do. I knew from experience that following only the voice of knowledge in my mind didn't often bring me happiness or put me on a good, healthy path. In fact, that voice of knowledge often led me down roads that I wish now I had not taken, or asked me to close doors that in hindsight I would have been better off walking though.

I prefer to call the combination of heart-voice, intuition, and mind my inner wisdom. I see them as distinct voices that give slightly different viewpoints on a person, situation, or decision. To me, in the best circumstances, they all work together in balance and harmony. At least they should, in theory. Some of us, though, have learned to listen to one of these three and ignore the other two. This was me: for years, I listened only to the voice of my mind and ignored my heart and intuition.

Listening to my intuition and heart is a different approach to living than I have allowed myself in the past. While I haven't abandoned logic or reasoning, I do make a real effort to put much more weight on the guidance of my heart and intuition now.

What has following my heart and intuition entailed?

The first step on this more heart-centered path was to leave the career I'd known for so long: science and technical writing. While it was an exceptional career and good source of income, it was time for me to explore something more creative. Even though employers and clients expressed their happiness with my abilities, I needed a change from this type of corporate writing, at least for a while. Instead, I felt it was time to devote myself to my painting career and develop different writing skills, such as this book. Since I was seventeen years old, I've painted part time but never really felt that my work was refined enough to market nationally. It was time to start, and this book is a project that Spirit asked me to tackle, so how could I say no?

Another step on my path was to change up the subject matter of my paintings a little. In reality, this wasn't a conscious decision. I simply allowed my heart to call me to a different subject matter: horses. I had owned and ridden horses as a child and always enjoyed their beauty and presence, but now they somehow wanted to weave their way into my art. I simply allowed it to happen. The spirit of the horse called me to create, so I allow the creation to flow. Sometimes it feels as though I am incidental to the process — that I am simply the holder of the brush, not the master architect of the painting. Perhaps this is simply the state to which most artists aspire: being in-spirit as a conduit of the muse.

Other steps on this path include:

- Speaking my truth to those around me, including myself, while maintaining kindness and compassion.
- Staying true to my own path even when others pressure me to take a diversion that doesn't feel right.
- Entering into any type of relationship with an open, trusting heart while using sound judgment.

What has happened during the first several months of my grand experiment?

The biggest changes so far occurred internally. I feel deeply that my life is on a very good path. I'm much happier with myself and my life's direction, I have less stress about my daily life and my future, and

I don't really worry anymore. Some of this may be due to meeting my maker while in surgery that day, but I think most is from knowing that my heart-centered decisions are now in alignment with who I *really* am at my core.

If I have an opportunity put in front of me now, I think about whether it feels "right" for me to pursue it. I do a gut-check, a heart-check, and a mind-check. Do they all agree? If not, why? What is each voice of wisdom trying to tell me?

The best scenario is if all three voices agree on the path ahead. If one doesn't agree, I spend time in contemplation. Am I feeling unfounded fear? Is there something about the situation I need to pay attention to? Why are my intuition, heart, and mind telling me different things?

If it does feel right and no one is going to get hurt, I do it.

One other benefit of living more from my heart and intuition is that my artistic creativity and productivity have skyrocketed. The decision to leave my technical job seems to have freed up my creative muse in a big way. I can't wait to get to the easel every day, ideas flow effortlessly (so many that I can't keep up), and my craft of painting is better than it's ever been. Many more opportunities related to my art are flowing to me easily and more quickly than I ever would have imagined, perhaps because I am living more in alignment with who I am meant to be.

And overall, I notice that I am more open, more buoyant, and, well, just plain happier. What's not to like about that?

When I Don't Listen

Not being a saint or a guru, I admit that listening to the calls of my heart and intuition feels difficult sometimes. My decision-making can still lean to following the voice of knowledge and ignoring my heart. I guess that shouldn't be a surprise since that's how I've lived most of my life. When my voice of knowledge demands to take over, some deep breaths and settling my mind will help me hear that quiet, inner voice of my heart. I've only ignored that heart-voice a couple of times in the last four months, and the experience that followed reminded me why I started on this path in the first place.

I know when I'm ignoring my inner wisdom, but especially my heart. I feel like my life is off-track, and I'll often feel vaguely uneasy or mildly anxious. In extreme situations, it seems as though everything is going wrong. When this happens, I try to step away from the situation with my mind and heart, and think about what's going on.

One recent time I ignored my inner wisdom was on a trip that I took to see some longtime friends in Idaho. The first part of my time away was wonderful. My friends and I had a great visit and it felt right to be connecting with them after many years apart. When I was due to leave Idaho and start driving back to Colorado, I had a choice to make about what to do with my limited time available. I needed to be home by a specific day so only had about four days available to me. My options included driving south into Utah for some hiking and artistic research, or I could head straight east to Rock Springs, WY, to spend a few days photographing the herds of wild horses in the area. My brain wanted me to go south into Utah. It made sense to try to shove as much research time as I could into this trip. My heart wanted to go straight to Rock Springs and photograph the horses. I decided to listen to my brain and go to Utah.

Big mistake.

As soon as I started on the Utah portion of my trip, it seemed as though everything went wrong. Torrential rains (uncommon in this very dry part of the west) prevented me from getting into most of the research sites I'd planned on visiting. Bull-headed as I was, I tried to see a couple of the areas anyway. After 15-plus miles of attempting to drive on a clay road that had turned into a slick quagmire, I decided that calling it quits and getting out of there was my safest option. I wasted three days battling the weather and deep mud before listening to my heart and finally driving up to Rock Springs, Wyoming. What happened there? A superbly magical time with the wild horse herds, just as my heart-voice was trying to tell me all along!

When I don't listen to my heart-voice now, I feel that I'm fighting against the flow of spiritual guidance. As in my story above, one thing after another seems to go wrong. Roadblocks keep popping up where knowledge and reason say that the path ahead should be clear. Things just don't *feel* or *work* right. That's when I take time to get quiet and listen to the wisdom of my inner voice.

In the words of my Guide:

> *"When you are on your right track, you may feel a sense of rightness, calm, knowing, or inner peace. This feeling is your guiding light. When you are off track, you may feel a sense of anxiety or simply know that something is not right in your life. Use these feelings to readjust your course on your life's path. Remember to temper this with your mind, though, for your mind is also a gift that you can use to balance your heart-voice."*

PRACTICE LISTENING TO YOUR INNER WISDOM

How can you listen to your heart, especially when that voice is often so quiet?

Since each person and each heart-voice is different, that's a tough question to answer. I'll give you some general approaches that have worked for me, but ultimately you will have to find your own way.

- *When confronted with a decision, a situation, or an event, do the three-part check.* What does your intuition or gut say to do? What does your heart or emotion say to do? And what does your mind tell you to do? Do they all agree? If not, why not?
- *Pay attention when you get a strong feeling (not a thought, but a feeling).* An example might be getting a strong feeling to take a different way home from work this evening. If following this feeling won't hurt anyone, try listening to it. What happens? Was your feeling

right? When I used to drive long distances on my daily commute, I would occasionally have a strong feeling to take a different way home from work. Almost always that little voice was correct so I learned to listen to it.

- *The more you listen to your inner wisdom and learn when and how often it's right, the more you'll "hear" it and pay attention to it.*
- *I've found that spending time in quiet meditation, contemplation, or prayer every day helps me to more easily hear my inner wisdom.* Try to have some daily time to quiet your mind so that you can tune in to your intuition and your heart. It can also help you calm your mind and figure out what it's trying to tell you. The heart and intuition speak when the mind is quiet. Try to find even five minutes a day to go on a quiet, contemplative walk, sit in a garden and clear your mind of your worries, or even join a meditation group. Sometimes exercise can induce a quiet-mind state: a walk, running, a bicycle ride, or maybe cross-country skiing is what you need. Try to build little moments of quiet-mind states into your day and see if that helps you tune in to your inner wisdom.
- *Cultivate quiet time at home.* I've noticed that my inner voice is enhanced when I make my home a quiet zone. I turn off all noise-making media and simply let my mind and muse wander in that quiet space. I realize this may not be easy for some people but give it a try. I don't have much data to back this up but my feeling is that the constant media assault on my senses dampens my unique inner voice, my creativity, and can increase my stress levels, which further quiets that inner wisdom. Personally, I don't have cable and watch very little TV. Just a few hours a week of science shows on PBS, a couple of episodes of my favorite cooking show, and that's about it. I rarely listen to TV news. If I want news, I read headlines and selected articles online or listen to National Public Radio (NPR). I would much rather spend my time with friends, being creative, writing, reading,

doing yoga, pondering my latest painting idea, or even watching the sunset. This quiet time allows both my mind and spirit some freedom to be themselves, to think and feel freely, without other influences.

CHAPTER 14

We Are Never Alone

WE ARE NEVER ALONE. *We are surrounded by love and the Divine constantly. Every second of every day, and even in our darkest hours, we are connected to Spirit.*

FULL MESSAGE

Many times during my tour through Heaven, I felt connected to other spiritual beings, including the Divine. They communicated to me, buoyed my soul, and made me feel welcomed and loved. I didn't feel intruded-upon, though, simply supported and loved. They wanted me to understand that I wasn't alone.

That interconnectedness to every being in Heaven was difficult to leave behind when I came back to Earth. Actually, it felt wrenching, a gaping hole where there had been a supportive love from many others. And being able to share love with the Divine presence in a way that I could *feel* seemed natural there. That deep, real-time connection to God was the most difficult thing to give up in coming back to Earth.

But what I learned is that even here, even now, we're all connected to Spirit. We're never alone. Through my Guide, they told me this before I was sent back, and they showed me a vision of spiritual beings surrounding me in my life as a human. They also showed me that I could cultivate connections to other people (in other words, make more friends) if I chose. And of course, they said, God was there for me any time of the day or night.

Here on Earth, how many people feel alone in life, or even lonely? If we go by findings published in the National Science Foundation's *General Social Survey*[25], approximately 50% of Americans feel they have no one to talk to about their troubles or accomplishments. Those who prefer isolation may not see this as a problem, but my guess is that most of us would like to have at least a small group of people to share life with.

We are surrounded by people but many feel stymied when it comes to making real, substantive connections with others. We may also feel isolated from our spirituality or spiritual source as well.

During my near-death experience, my Guide showed me that we don't *need* to feel isolated and lonely if what we crave is friendship and connection. Reaching out and connecting with others is a choice we have. We can choose to build communities of friendship and support around us.

If we're feeling lonely, we can set fear aside and make a conscious decision to take action to reach out to others. We can also strengthen our connection to Spirit. This might not be easy at first[26], especially for those who have years of alone-time under their belts. But if we crave a fulfilling life of joyful connection, reaching out to forge bonds with others and develop our spirituality is a necessary first step on that path. I'll discuss human connections a bit later, but let's start by considering a more expansive and grander connection — the connection to our spiritual source.

CONNECTION TO SPIRIT

Through being in Heaven, I simply understood *somehow* that the realm of Spirit really isn't a separate place that we travel *to* when we die; in

---

25 McPherson, M., Smith-Lovin, L., and Brashears, M., "General Social Survey." *American Sociological Review*, June 2006, vol. 71 no. 3.

26 If you feel profoundly lonely, down, depressed, or have thoughts of suicide, please reach out to a psychological or medical professional, a trusted friend, or call the National Suicide Prevention Lifeline at 1-800-273-8255.

large part, it's simply a shift of "state" *and it is here all around us right now.* Our connection to God is available to us all of the time. Heaven isn't a physical place. It's a state of being that we can call out to any time.

That's why I say that we're never alone, and that's one reason why my Guide felt sadness when we feel loneliness or isolation. Spiritual love flows around us constantly. God is beside us, behind us, and in front of us. He's got our backs.

Spirit exists in our hearts, always. We simply need to be still, mentally or emotionally, to feel that presence, to experience that love within us.

The Divine never abandons us. We might turn away from Him, but that's our choice. We always have the option to turn away or to come home. Sometimes that loving voice is quiet in our lives, but "quiet" doesn't mean "gone." Spirit's methods of communication to us can be subtle, even hidden or indirect.

For example, the job you didn't get is the one where your potential boss will be indicted for embezzling in three months. God's got your back.

Spirit is there for you when your fiancé cancels the wedding at the last minute. Years later you find out that she has had a drug addiction, but hid it from you.

God's presence is with you when you are feeling lonely, too. It's there in the smile of a stranger passing you on the street or the helping hand from someone you just met on your first day in a new job. It's there in the produce stockist who goes out of her way to get you those beautiful tomatoes to make your salad extra special for your anniversary dinner.

God is there in the hug from your child, the friendly hello from someone in the grocery store, and in the ecstatic wag of a tail from your dog when you come home.

That Divine love is with you. Walk with an open and accepting heart to see it at work.

Spirit is also with us in the moment when we see the gorgeous sunset over the mountains, in the first crocus of spring, in the hummingbird that just visited a flower garden. He is there with us in the sweet scent of a rose, in the call of a Meadowlark, and in the deep blue sky of a sunny summer's day.

We don't have to look very hard. Slow down. Pay attention and you can experience that loving presence everywhere.

So many of us don't *want* to find our spiritual connection, or don't know how. We might shut it down or refuse to feel it in our lives. We constantly drown out God's voice with our electronics and portable music when we're out in nature. We may push Spirit away by isolating ourselves — by choosing computers and text messages over seeing friends face-to-face. A computer can't give us hugs when we need them, but a friend can when we see her in person. And in that friend's hug is a hug from Spirit too.

Some of us have lost the knowledge of God's existence in our lives, yet long for it.

Make an effort to find the Divine in all of those quiet spaces. Try to hear that loving voice in your heart, feel the presence of love in your soul. See if you can spot Spirit in your newborn's eyes. Such incredible potential for love wrapped up in such a small bundle! You may see a spiritual presence in those sunflower seeds you're planting, too. Those little seeds will burst forth with incredible energy and fervor and in a few short weeks you will have some of the biggest, most brilliant flowers in your garden! A true miracle. All from a small bundle of almost-nothing.

It is a miracle. And yes, it's biology too. Science and Spirit work together, not in opposition.

My Guide also asked that we don't forget about those who have passed on before us. When you have an open heart and call on them to help, they will be there. In fact, they are among us when we least expect it. We might not see or hear them with our human senses, but they are here. It can be just the memory a loved one has left behind that helps you. It can be the things they taught, their positive presence, or their loving influence that lives on in your life. And some may believe that it's their soul that lives on and helps us when we need it most. Have you felt the presence of a lost loved one in your life?

Those who touched our lives are here to lend us love and support that we may be able to feel it even if we are not consciously aware of it. They are a part of our spiritual community and enjoy encouraging us, giving us energy or guidance when we need it, and cheering us on in their own way. They love watching our lives unfold, too.

And they are also with us when we take our last breaths of life, to welcome us back home.

So you see, we're never alone. Spirit in all its forms is with us, in us, all of the time.

Community

Earlier in this chapter I mentioned the importance of connecting with others. My Guide and I both believe that in order to live truly fulfilled and joyous lives, building a community of support around us is vitally important. Humans aren't meant to exist in isolation. Friends, church, work, and family can all be good starting points to establish and experience a sense of community.

But our communities are active. We must continually cultivate them much as we would cultivate and nurture a garden. Seedlings will wither if not watered properly. So too will our communities of support if we ignore them. We must actively participate in the lives of our friends and loved ones, we must lend a hand when others need help, and also allow them to help us if we're to build a strong center of support.

When we're actively cultivating our own communities of friends and support around us, we're taking proactive steps to prevent ourselves from falling into the traps of loneliness and isolation. Reach out. Open yourself to the presence of others. Open your heart and life to friends and family. Allow others into your life so that you don't need to be alone.

See Chapter 12 for more on building communities of support.

MY THOUGHTS

The months prior to my crash found me at one of the loneliest points in my life.

I'd felt worse only once before — the year after my divorce was a tough one in all respects. Getting used to being alone wasn't easy. I'd grown up in a busy household on a small farm, surrounded by parents, siblings, friends, and critters both wild and domestic. My early life overflowed with the energy and love of both people and nature. In a profound way, this was a slice of Heaven for me.

In my early forties, I divorced my husband and for a long time I lived alone. By the autumn prior to my accident I often felt lonely and disconnected, even though overall I thought I was "OK" with being single. I had come to like my own company and enjoy my quiet time, but still I had a vague sense of loneliness. I thought at issue was the fact that it had been many years since my divorce and still I hadn't found a healthy romantic relationship. It turns out that was only partly the problem.

Most of the feelings of loneliness and isolation were my own fault. For a variety of reasons, I've not been the gregarious sort — hanging out in smoke-filled singles bars or loud dance clubs was not my idea of fun. I preferred spending time with small groups of friends, participating in clubs related to my interests or hobbies, or volunteering for various non-profits. But in those months before my accident I seemed to intentionally withdraw from the social activities I *did* enjoy. I stopped participating in the cycling club I'd belonged to, and quit the organized hikes I'd often attended. I didn't go to the chamber orchestra concerts I usually enjoyed and even avoided spending time with some of my longtime friends.

At the time, I did notice my pulling back but couldn't put my finger on why I felt the need to do this. In hindsight, I think most of the loneliness and isolation was the result of living against my nature — spending years as a staunch atheist — when in my heart I felt differently. My atheistic viewpoint was a rebellion of sorts. I rebelled against my Roman

Catholic upbringing by denying spirituality altogether. And in a university science curriculum, atheism was the norm so I followed that pattern without giving it much thought.

My guess is that a long-term disconnection from my spiritual center finally got the better of me.

When I heard this message from my Guide, that *we are never really alone*, I wept with the knowledge, beauty, and feeling in that simple statement. My angst and stress about my loneliness released in a flood of tears. It was more than a simple statement of words, though. She flooded my *being* with images, feelings, and love to go with the words.

I saw my family, friends, and coworkers in life. She showed me my family members who had passed on, and how they still visited me in my life. I saw almost-invisible energy connections to spiritual beings who wanted to help me or lend me their love. And I saw my connection of love to God, a connection that never goes away.

She forced me to come face-to-face with Divine love, and that understanding filled my soul with profound joy — a joy that still reverberates through me whenever I have the need or desire for it.

The truth was always hiding in plain sight: *we are never alone.*

No matter how much we shut ourselves off from Spirit, that loving energy is still with us, waiting for us to call upon it. No matter how many barriers we build, how many times we feel hurt, how much we pull away from it, that love is always there, ready to welcome us home when we gather up the courage to reach out.

I'd never been much of a student of the Christian faith but I re-read the parable of the Prodigal Son recently. It's beautiful. That story really is what it's like when we choose to "come home" to Spirit. When we acknowledge our connection to that loving presence, when we open our arms to the light, the love of the Divine is there, waiting for us to come home. We don't have to die to experience it. It's there for us, right now.

Accountability

When I fully understood that God is with us *all of the time*, it scared me at first. Understanding deep down that I really can't hide, that *no matter where I go Spirit is here with me*, made me feel a little bit like Big Brother was watching. I felt self-conscious about everything.

The larger concept, though, is the understanding that we really can't hide our actions, thoughts, and words from ourselves, our communities, or God. While I wasn't taught about the existence of a hell, I did learn that we are held accountable for our actions in many ways, and some that may not be obvious to us at first.

My Guide explained to me that what we say, think, and do sends out very real "energies" from our core *being*. Some might call these vibrations or "vibes." These energies consist of body language, words, actions, thoughts, and even spiritual energy. If your words and actions are fearful or negative, the energies that your personality gives off are fearful and negative. What you attract will likely also be only fearful and negative people or things. How many positive, loving people want to hang around someone who is negative and fearful? Not many.

It's similar to how ripples on a pond travel outward from the source. You are a source of actions, words, feelings, and thoughts, and those travel outward from you in energies similar to waves.

On a more practical note, if your mind is fully committed to fear or negativity, it's closed to anything good or positive that may be happening in your surroundings. You voluntarily close yourself off to experiencing the good by staying mired in your fear or negative thoughts, and your negative cycle continues.

The opposite is also true. The more we send out love, strength, goodness, and light in our words and actions, the stronger is the field of love around us. We send those positive waves outward into those around us. Love is strong, so if we cultivate it just a bit more than fear and negativity, the love can overpower those "lesser" energies. Also, when your being is more entrenched in positive thinking and feeling, you are more likely to see additional, positive experiences in your life. On a practical note, our minds will be more open to noticing and experiencing more of the positive people and things around us if we are in a positive mindset.

Our thoughts, words, and actions also have an effect on our lives in ways we may have heard of as "karma" or "what you sow, so shall you reap." What we put out, we do get back but not necessarily in another lifetime. It can come back to us rather quickly! If you own a business and are rude or unresponsive to your customers, what happens to your business? In all likelihood your business will suffer. Conversely, if you treat your customers with respect and gratitude, give them a good product, and are responsive to their needs, what happens? It's more likely that your business will do well.

The same is true in our personal lives. Who wants to hang around obnoxious, negative, mean people all of the time? I certainly don't. Understand that if you're sending out negative, mean-spirited energy, you may be driving people away. Conversely, if your energies are mostly positive and upbeat, you will more likely attract positive and upbeat people who want to hang out with someone like them.

I'd rather be with people who are mostly upbeat, fun, positive, and caring. This is one reason I try to stay conscious of the energies I'm sending out into the world. I intend to attract fun, positive, helpful, and compassionate people into my life so one way to do that is to *be* fun, positive, helpful, and compassionate most of the time.

I'm not perfect, though. I slip up, get in a funk or a mental rut, and have to pull myself back up again. Sometimes friends or loved ones help me see this. Sometimes I see it myself. When this happens, I spend time thinking about why I got into the funk. Is there something I need to learn? Could I be doing something differently? What changes can I make to put myself back in the positive mental and emotional state that is best for me? What can I do so that I feel more peaceful?

The energies we send out directly influence the people around us, which in turn comes back into our lives. If you're feeling lonely and isolated, think about what's going on in your life? Are you inadvertently doing or saying things that drive others away? Are you sending out signals that say you don't want companionship, friendship, or love?

It's not easy to examine ourselves in this way. We may not want to realize that we're being our own worst enemies, but this type of questioning may help us start to make positive changes in our lives and in the lives of those we care for.

It's not rocket science or magic. Think about it for a moment. What you put out, you *do* get back.

Community

Another piece of the puzzle related to positive, loving energy is the reminder my Guide gave me to open my arms and heart to *my own* communities, here and now on Earth. As humans, we evolved to live in small, close-knit groups. While most of us don't live in tribes anymore, the effort to form "tribes" or communities around us can pay us back tenfold in love and support.

These communities can be anything that fills our need for connection: family, friends, friendly coworkers, members of clubs we belong to, members of our religious or spiritual centers, even neighbors can become part of our community. And sometimes that community expands to include people we don't even know but who lend a hand when there is a need.

For us to feel truly fulfilled and happy, I believe it's necessary for us to have at least some of these connections in person. Often times, the support we most need comes from those who will physically be there for us when we experience troubles. Social media friends are nice to have, but most of them can't help you out if your car gets stuck in a snowdrift or you literally need a shoulder to cry on.

My accident showed me just how valuable these personal connections are.

At the time of my accident, most of my family lived out of state. I had one niece about an hour away, but my siblings were scattered across the USA. Consequently, the first people to come to support me in the hospital were friends and coworkers who lived close by. Their presence so quickly after my accident let me know that I wasn't alone, that I was cared for, and that I had people who would be there to help me through what lay ahead. Having these friends and coworkers appear to hold my hand helped me feel that I was truly supported and didn't need to be alone. Even though my body hurt, my heart felt warm and glowing from their presence.

At the time of the crash, I worked at a small software company in Boulder, Colorado. For those who don't know Boulder, it has a reputation for being a mecca of elite professional and amateur athletes. Cyclists, rock climbers, trail runners, mountaineers, and adventure athletes of all kinds seem to make up 80% of the population. Scientists or software engineers by day turn into serious athletic warriors after 5 PM. My coworkers were no exception. When they heard the news that I'd been struck by a vehicle while I was riding my bicycle, they couldn't step up fast enough to help. Not only was I a coworker, I was a member of the local cycling community. The accident could have happened to any one of them! Not only did several of them visit me in the hospital, they helped me as I recuperated at home too. Once I came home, they delivered food and meals to me for six weeks, helped out around my home, bought and delivered little things that I needed to make life easier, donated vacation time to me, and most importantly, worked at keeping my spirits up.

This was something I really didn't expect and because of that, their generosity brought tears to my eyes many times. While I liked my coworkers and enjoyed being in the office, only a very few of them had become close friends. But almost everyone in my department helped out in one way or another — even those I had rarely worked with and barely knew. The outpouring of support from this very unexpected community still chokes me up today, nearly ten months later. I finally felt that knowledge soar through me: I am not alone.

My Guide reminded me that community is something we can and should cultivate around us, and not just for support in the hard times like I experienced. We feel better when we are part of a group that cares for each other and has fun together. But it's an active thing. We have to get out of our routine, go on walks or hikes with friends, have a group potluck, crack jokes, discuss the meaning of life, or watch sports or movies together. Whatever your thing is, get some folks together and just do it.

If the thought of that is difficult for you, start slowly. Make a commitment to reach out and connect with a friend you haven't seen in a while. Make that phone call. Meet for lunch or beers or to watch a sports team play on the weekend. Get together to have a Star Trek or NCIS marathon.

Make a commitment to reach out to just one person this week and see how it feels.

Practice Reaching Out

Opening your heart and mind to your spiritual source will be a very personal journey. I can't tell you how to do it. I can only tell you how I cultivate this connection now that I know it's there.

- *I make silent time every day to receive any insights Spirit chooses to share with me.* This sometimes coincides with an activity such as walking, hiking, or driving, but not always. I simply try to let the chatter of my mind fall away and focus on my surroundings without letting specific thoughts form about what I'm experiencing. Oftentimes, solutions to problems will come to me, and insights will appear as if out of nowhere.
- *Yes, I'm human and I do get angry or sad sometimes, so I express it.* Sometimes I get very frustrated and make demands for clarity or a resolution from spiritual source, and the clarity often comes to me with all of the force of my initial frustration! If I'm adamant,

impatient, and forceful, it's mirrored back to me. I think Spirit has a sense of humor.

- *Every day, I make an effort to see love and beauty reflected in my surroundings.* When I'm on a walk, I'll notice an elderly couple shuffling around the park, holding hands, obviously longtime partners. I'll see the love they have for each other and give thanks that I'm blessed to be witnessing it. Often, seeing love so tangibly expressed like this brings me to tears. I can also experience Divine presence just by opening my heart to nature when I'm on a hike or driving through a beautiful landscape. I take a moment to appreciate nature's gifts and express gratitude for the opportunity to experience it.
- *I feel and express gratitude to the people I encounter in my daily life.* Remember, gratitude is a form of love, so in expressing it I feel connected not only to those around me, but to my spiritual source as well.

CHAPTER 15

Choice

---

*ULTIMATELY, OUR MOST POWERFUL TOOL **for this life is the power of choice over our thoughts, words, and actions. Used wisely and with compassion, choice is our most incredible gift and tool for living the lives we want.***

FULL MESSAGE

One of the strongest visuals my Guide gave me during my time in Heaven centered around the power that we have in the choices we make. It came as we walked along a creek in a little valley that wound among some ancient-looking, worn-down mountains. I gazed at the mountains and trees, enjoying the peaceful scene. Then we happened upon a small pond. Its water was dark and deep, and a few colorful leaves floated on its surface. My Guide instructed me to kneel by the water's edge. When I did, I sensed this wasn't an ordinary pond. She asked me to gently touch the surface to see what happened. Well, it was a pond, I knew what would happen but I followed her instruction anyway. By now I knew to simply do as I was told.

Ripples emanated outward from the place I touched the water. The leaves moved up and down in response to the ripples that moved under them. But superimposed on the ripples I saw the choices that I'd made in my life. Those choices, like the ripples, made little waves in the world around me. They affected other people. They affected my future. And they somehow affected my past, too. Good or bad, my choices had an impact.

This visual comes to me often now that I'm back here in my human life. I keep that pond in mind when I'm about to make an important decision, when I speak in front of a group, or even when I talk with family or friends. My choices have an impact. I'm not powerless.

One of the gifts that we have as adults is the power to choose, to make decisions, and to direct our own lives. We can choose how to think and act. We can choose the words we use. We can decide to follow the Light or turn towards darkness. It's all up to us.

Yet many of us feel powerless. Things happen that seem out of our control. We watch the news and are bombarded with tragic events we can do nothing about. But we do have incredible power, even if we don't see it right away. We have the power to change the world immediately around us through the effective use of our own thoughts, words, feelings, and actions.

If we choose to use all of these carefully, with love in our hearts and positive intentions, we can have powerfully positive lives. But if we make choices with an uninformed, negative, or malicious state of mind, or with negative intent and not aligned with Spirit, our choices can easily hurt or destroy ourselves or others.

We can also use our thoughts, feelings, words, and actions to help bring people, things, or events into our lives. Some may call this "manifesting." When all four (thoughts, feelings, words, and actions) are mostly in alignment with each other, with Spirit, and with who we are inside, the things that come to us tend to be positive and we are more able to deflect or deal with negative things. But if those thoughts, feelings, words, and actions are not in alignment with Spirit or our own natures, we may send out energies that seem to somehow attract negativity into our lives.

How can this be?

Remember that pond? Everything we do, including the words we speak, our actions, and thoughts, has an effect on both ourselves and the world around us. We can liken these effects to energy radiating outward from our centers. Our words and actions do not affect just us, they travel outward and touch others, too. And the sphere of that impact can be quite large.

For example, if you would like a fun new friend to come into your life but your mindset and actions project negativity and anger, you probably won't be attractive to the kind of person you're seeking. Conversely, if you are acting from a state of fun, with loving-kindness and compassion, you will be much more attractive to a new friend who's also a joy to be with.

My Guide stated this many times but I think it bears repeating. A negative state of mind is not just something that *we* hold on to. It can easily affect others. When our minds stay mired in negativity, we may snap at our families, use harsh words, or perhaps even lash out physically without really thinking.

Similarly, a positive state of mind has a positive sphere of influence radiating out from us. If we are in a positive, happy mindset, how we treat others will doubtless reflect that. We will probably treat others in a positive way by using kind words, doing good things, and being helpful and compassionate.

Does this make us responsible for everyone out there? No. We each are accountable for our own selves first and foremost. If we have young children or other dependents, we are responsible for them as well, *to a point.*[27] But Spirit wants us to begin to understand how our words and actions might affect those around us and eventually, come back into our own lives.

Put another way, while we can't control the actions of others, we should realize that *our actions can and do affect others and eventually, ourselves.*

This bit of Navajo wisdom explains it beautifully:

---

27 As I've written earlier, we have the responsibility to raise and care for our children in the best way accessible to us. But spiritually-speaking, we're not responsible for telling them how to live their lives once they become adults.

"Thoughts are like arrows: once released, they strike their mark. Guard them well or one day you may be your own victim."

While I agree with this, I would add that words and actions are like arrows, too. All of them can come back to help or harm us later.

Ripples on a Pond

Let's go back to that pond. Our thoughts, words, feelings, and actions travel out from us as ripples on a pond travel outward from the drop of a pebble on its surface. It doesn't matter whether our thoughts, words, feelings, and actions are positive or negative, they still travel outward from us. If a leaf is floating on the surface of that pond, it will move in response to the energy of the ripple that passes under it. It's all energy, radiating out from its source and interacting with all it comes in contact with.

Our words and actions affect others and the world around us, just as those ripples moved the leaf on the surface of the pond. Consistently sending out negative thoughts, words, feelings, and actions perpetuates the negativity, which can then pass on to others. The same is true of positive (non-destructive) words and actions. They can uplift and encourage those around us, as well as ourselves. In some instances they can even offset negativity from others.

Think about two pebbles dropped into a pond but separated by ten feet or so. Ripples on the pond's surface travel outward from each pebble in a generally circular pattern. But at some point the ripples from one pebble impact the ripples from the second and they interact. Where they interact, they can either cancel each other out or make a bigger ripple. This is called interference or magnification, depending on how the ripples interact.

When positive ripples from us come in contact with other positive ripples from others, the effect is magnified. Similarly, negative ripples can magnify each other and become even more negative. And when positive ripples from you come into negative ripples from another? Well, the positive can cancel out or even overwhelm the negative and change the dynamic of the surface of the "pond." What was negative can be made more positive.

We can equate this to negative *vs.* positive words and actions. Here's a simple example: within your circle of friends, several get together for a party. One of your friends is angry and snapping at everyone she sees. She and her boyfriend just had a serious argument and she carries that anger to your gathering. Her negative emotion travels outward from her like those ripples on a pond. But you and your other friends are feeling good and having a wonderful time. You speak positive words to each other and act in loving, compassionate ways to all, including your angry friend. Your positive words and actions travel outward from all of you, just like more ripples on that pond. And because you and your friends are stronger in your positive thoughts and words, they overwhelm or offset much if not all of the negativity your angry friend felt and sent out. In fact, you help boost her spirits and mood. She eventually goes home and has a productive talk with her boyfriend that helps settle their argument.

My Guide also told me about the more subtle effects from our thoughts and feelings.

What you think and feel inside your mind is the engine that drives the words and actions that emanate from you. This makes sense. Our thoughts and feelings are the drivers for what we do and say, after all. This a very direct way that thoughts and feelings become "real" in our world.

If we have thoughts of paranoia, that everyone is out to do us harm, those thoughts may cause us to withdraw or lash out, to take a negative action, or speak negatively. The fear we carry impacts our interaction with others in a negative way, possibly reinforcing our feelings of paranoia and making it even bigger in our minds.

If our thoughts and feelings are mostly positive, our words and actions will follow suit and positively impact our immediate world. When we are thinking positive thoughts and feeling good inside, our words and actions cannot help but to fall into alignment and we'll have a positive impact on the world around us. The reach of our thoughts may be small, it may just be our families, friends, and coworkers, but *any* positive impact is significant. Our coworkers in turn have an impact on their circle too, and so on, and in that way our initial, small, positive impact can radiate outward to a larger area. Our positive thoughts and actions can move across a population, a little at a time, and they can build on each other.

Ripples Across the World

Remember that when in-phase ripples interact on the surface of a pond, the height of the resulting ripple gets bigger? In the same way, positive words and actions can build on each other as they are passed from one person to the next. Your kind words to a stranger may have been just the thing she needed in that moment to lift her spirits after a business deal went sour. Your words lifted her spirits and later allowed her to successfully close an even larger deal. She decides that because she feels good from the second deal, she will make a large financial donation to a charity that provides health care to those who need it. Your relatively small words of kindness were just multiplied into a much bigger, positive impact.

We really never know how a kind word or deed can affect the world around us.

Some of you might protest that you cannot control your thoughts and you definitely cannot control your feelings.

Not true.

With practice, you *can* have more control over your thoughts.[28] I won't say that it's easy, and I won't guarantee 100% control over your

---

28 See the books of Dr. Daniel Amen on ways to control ANTs (Automatic Negative Thoughts). His series on "Change Your Brain..." are especially helpful. Or check in with a counselor or therapist if you're besieged by negative thoughts and feelings.

thinking, but it is very possible to be more in control of what's happening in your mind. Don't give negative thoughts fertile ground to take root. Stamp them out as soon as you notice them. Replace them with something positive. It can be simply a gorgeous image, like a beautiful flower, or something uplifting that you want to bring into your life.

Your mind and thinking are complex. They can seem like a herd of stampeding wildebeest at times but you *can* bring them under more control. Ultimately, with practice, you can learn to direct the majority of your thoughts toward those you want. The first step is being aware of what you are thinking. Once you are aware, then you have the option to make a change.

And in a similar way, you can master control of your feelings.

PRACTICAL MANIFESTING

I won't get into the details of manifesting here. So many other authors have already broached this topic that I'm not sure I can add anything substantial.[29] But some of the things my Guide taught me *do* have an impact on how we can bring people, events, or things into our lives.

From a very practical point of view, manifesting isn't magic or rocket science and is linked to our thoughts, feelings, words, and actions in a very physical and rational way. If you're mired in negativity, speak angry words, or act in destructive ways, people will tend to steer clear of you even if you want connection. You will drive positive, happy, loving people away. The only people who might want to be with you are also people who are mired in negativity.

If you are positive, happy, and loving, people will tend to be attracted to you. You'll find many more opportunities to connect with others than if you were stuck in negativity.

In the bigger picture, living with your thoughts, feelings, words, and actions in alignment with your core self allows you to focus your energies

---

29 For an easy-to-understand guide on manifesting, see Ken Elliott's book, *Manifesting 1-2-3*.

clearly on what you want. You can easily channel more of yourself into achieving your goals. And when you know what you want, are able to focus on it, devote energy to it, you're more likely to *get* what you want.

Think about a young boy who wants to be an Olympic-caliber runner. If he thinks about running, feels he can achieve it, is excited about his goal, immerses himself in the sport, practices, eats healthfully, visualizes himself achieving his goal, gets a good coach, etc., he is much more likely to achieve his goal than a boy who does none of these things.

Think about what you can do to align your thoughts, feelings, words, and actions with what you want to bring into your life.

From a more spiritual viewpoint, manifesting deals with energy. The realm of Spirit is, at its core, energetic. Its structure is the energy of love. Divine love permeates and forms the structure of everything. *Everything*. There is nowhere that love is not. I saw and experienced this quite vividly while I was near death.

Let that sink in for a moment.

Here's the kicker: *the core or structure of our physical world is also the energy of spiritual love.* Our physical realm contains a loving energy at its core. Love helps to form the structure of our world just as love forms the structure of spirituality. We have the added layer of "physical-ness" here, but at its core, everything contains the energy of love.

Since our thoughts, feelings, words, and actions emanate from us as energy, they can positively or negatively impact the loving energy that forms the world around us too, just like the ripples on the pond affect a leaf floating on its surface.

Dealing With Outside Events

What about outside events? We can't control everything in our lives. Unexpected things do happen. Unforeseen events can make us veer from our goals for a short time, or forever, even if our thoughts, feelings, words, and actions line up. Stuff happens.

How do we handle this?

Allow yourself time to grieve, to adjust to the changes, to think about what happened, perhaps learn from the situation, readjust your plan, or to set a new course. Even if something negative happens to you or someone you love, that doesn't mean that you're somehow at fault or are a bad person.

The key is in building your own inner well of resiliency. Call on a friend. Call on Spirit. You're not alone.

Understand that you don't need to react in a negative way. Remember that you still maintain the power over your thoughts, feelings, words, and actions. Take some time to mentally and emotionally deal with the event. Reach out for help. Get advice from a counselor or spiritual advisor if you have trouble dealing with the setback yourself. Then choose how to proceed in as positive a way as you can.

Maybe that means you let go of one goal and reset your course to another. Learn from the setback. Don't take it personally. Evaluate your options, make adjustments to your life, then step out on your new path.

Life awaits you.

My Thoughts

I never really paid much attention to how powerful words, actions, thoughts, and feelings were until my Guide drilled this one home for me with the visual metaphor of the pond ripples.

Like so many people, I lived much of my younger years unconsciously, on autopilot, not fully present in the moment and mostly out of touch with my actual thoughts, feelings, words, and actions. I often didn't pay attention to how someone reacted to my words — not because I didn't want to, but because I'd never learned to make that a part of my consciousness. When I did pay attention and realized I'd caused distress, I didn't have the communication skills to fix things. I lived much of that time in sort of a dream-state, disconnected both from my own inner self and the people around me. I just didn't know any better.

I cringe now at some of the decisions I made, like staying in a relationship too long because I didn't want to be alone. I'm sure most of us have made decisions like that. As I grew older, my life skills improved, but not as much as I would have liked. I still hurt people unintentionally by acting out or speaking without thinking, and I continued to live parts of my life on autopilot. Today this strikes me as very odd since I've spent most of my working years as a communications professional. I excelled at business and technical communication, but stunk when it came to interpersonal interactions. Go figure.

Things changed when I learned that I could choose my thoughts, feelings, words, and actions, even if traumatic events happened to me. I could choose to make lemonade from lemons.

The Power in Conscious Choice

Every day that we're here on this Earth we make choices. We make choices when we interact with others and the world around us. We can build someone up or tear them apart with just a few words. We can improve our environment or ruin it, depending on the actions we take. With each choice we have an opportunity to project positive energies or negative, to reach for the light or the darkness.

It's up to us.

I know that we can't remain conscious one hundred percent of the time. I'm not a saint. I have unhealthy moments at times. But if I make a concerted effort to project more positive than negative energy, to walk more in the Light than in the Dark, the world around me will steadily become a much better place.

This is the power that my Guide referred to: the power we each have to influence the world around us.

You might think that one person's choices can't influence the world *all that much*, but you'd be wrong. With a seemingly simple decision to stay in her seat on a public bus in Montgomery, Alabama, Rosa Parks helped to launch the civil rights movement in the USA and raise the consciousness of an entire nation.

Our choices won't necessarily have a scope as large as hers but that doesn't mean they're not important. How we treat each other in our daily lives can have ripple effects that travel outward in ways we can't even fathom.

Let's not forget the importance of the energies we carry with us and project outward, even when we don't speak or act. Have you ever been in the presence of someone truly special, someone who can raise the positive energy in a room just by his or her presence? A person such as this seems to send out positive, calming, loving energy without saying a word.

My Own Choices

What choices have I made in my life after my accident, and what kinds of energy am I sending out?

In the first week or so after my accident, I will be the first to admit that my emotions flew out of control. The first few days, I felt anger at the poor choices of the woman who hit me. On top of the anger, or perhaps more correctly, at its core, I was terrified that my life as I knew it was over. I wept with fear that my active, outdoors-centered life would change drastically, that I would never regain my mental functioning, and that I'd be in constant pain for the rest of my life.

Then one day late in that first week, I realized could stop reacting to my circumstances and choose one of two paths before me: I could continue to live in a mental space of fear and anger and thus ruin any chance of living a happy life, or I could choose to learn from the positive aspects of my experience and go forward in a positive, compassionate frame of mind.

Viktor Frankl's book, *Man's Search for Meaning*, played a huge part in my emotional recovery after my accident. I remember reading about his finding beauty and meaning while in a World War II concentration camp.

I thought that if he could choose to live in beauty and feel love during those heinous times, then I could too. As I lay in my hospital bed thinking I might die, Frankl's finding beauty in fish heads floating in dirty water, kept me going. I knew then that my mind and spirit would be OK no matter what happened to my body. If Viktor Frankl could do it, I could, too.

In that moment I made my choice to live in love, to see beauty, and to find meaning and purpose in my hardships.

Since that time, my inner peace, happiness, and joy in life increases almost daily. I love myself, my life, and the people and world around me. Friends remark that my energy is very different: more upbeat, positive, peaceful, and joy-filled now.

Have I forgiven the woman driving the truck? I don't think "forgiveness" is the right word to use. I never wished her ill or harm. My only desire was, and still is, for her to learn to make better decisions in her life, to find happiness, to be a positive role model for her children, and to live in beauty.

Practice Healthy Choices

We can all choose to live more fully from a place of love and beauty, and to share that energy with the rest of the world. It's been said that music can soothe the savage beast. I guess that may be true, but practicing love, grace, and gratitude more often than not can also bring soothing energy to ourselves and those around us. We don't have to be gurus or saints, and we certainly don't need to be perfect, we only need to choose the path of love more often than not.

How?

Again, this is one of those areas where I can't exactly tell you how to live from a more conscious, intentional place and make positive choices,[30] I can only tell you some of the things that are working for me:

---

[30] Thich Nhat Hahn has written many books on mindfulness that may be helpful in learning to live consciously. Other authors in this area include the Dalai Lama, Eckhardt Tolle, Holly Sprink, and Deepak Chopra.

- *I try to listen more attentively and talk less these days when in conversation with another person.* I try to be as fully *present* in my interactions with others as possible. That means I keep my mind and emotions focused on the other person and what she is saying, rather than letting it drift to what I want to say, what I need to do later that afternoon, or the things I need to pick up at the grocery store.
- *I make a concerted effort to pause and think before I speak or act, considering how my words or actions might affect the other person or situation.*
- *I try to live consciously as much as I can.* As soon as I realize my mind and body are on autopilot, I stop, gather my thoughts, and put myself back in the present moment. This isn't easy and I'm not always successful, but I know that with continued practice it will become more natural.
- *I realize that mindfulness or living more intentionally is a journey rather than a destination.* I'm not expecting to be perfect, I simply try to get better and better all the time.
- *I stay mindful during activities like going for a walk.* I pay attention to the little things around me as much as possible, try to keep my mind on the present moment, and put my worries/fears on hold.
- *I live from an active space of gratitude and grace as much as I can.* I say "thank you" as often as I feel gratitude during the day. At the end of the day, I write down or recite aloud at least three things that I am grateful for that day. I also think about all of the good that happened, and ponder what I can learn from the not-so-good things that came into my life that day (if there are any).
- *I practice loving compassion and kindness as much as possible every day,* both to others and to myself.
- *I remember that this is a practice.* The more I practice being present, mindful, conscious, and gracious, the more it becomes second nature.

CHAPTER 16

Live Your Life Fully

───❦───

*You have one and only **one chance at life as the person you are now. Just one chance. Live your life to its fullest each day, spend your time wisely, and allow yourself to truly feel what it means to be alive as you. Please don't squander this gift. Live your life to its fullest as an expression of gratitude and love.***

Full Message

I've seen that what comes after the lives we have now is unimaginably wonderful. I glimpsed just a small bit of it and even with that peek, didn't want to come back here to Earth. The place we might call Heaven is filled with all-encompassing love and beauty. It truly is amazing, but so are these lives we have on this Earth, right now.

Our lives are huge gifts to be enjoyed, savored, and lived completely. No matter your religious or spiritual beliefs, *you have only one chance to live life as the beautiful person you are now.*

Think about that for a moment.

Even if you believe in some form of reincarnation, you are only *this* you, once.

Please don't waste this chance to savor your amazing life in all its nuances. Live your life wisely, lovingly, respectfully, and responsibly, but also fully in whatever way that means to you. Don't allow fear or others' desires for your life to stand in the way of making your life truly spectacular.

Perhaps your heart pulls you toward being a teacher, a lawyer, a minister, or even a jockey. Maybe you have a passion for piano, skiing, diving, training dogs, or creating terra cotta sculptures. Live those dreams and passions as fully as you can! You have only this one chance as the person you are now to make those dreams a reality.

God doesn't want us to put off living special, glorious lives on the promise of a beautiful "Heaven" ahead. Doing that is a waste of all the opportunity that the Creator has given us now on Earth. We are to live our dreams and lives fully, as best as we can, intentionally, with mindfulness, and in glorious homage to love.

We don't need to wait for Heaven to experience love and beauty. We can create our own slice of Heaven in our lives right now, and in doing so, we can bring a little of it into the lives of others too.

How wonderful is that?

By choosing to live with love and in beauty, we can bring a little bit of Heaven into the lives of those around us. If we choose to live this way, what could happen? Imagine the possibilities.

Our joy and happiness may infuse others whose lives we touch. We could bring joy into the lives of our families, friends, and even coworkers besides filling our own lives with joy. We might also inspire others to step out into the unknown and live their lives fully too. We could be the catalyst that a friend needs to leave her abusive husband, to finish a long-ignored university degree, or take that dream trip to Chile. We might inspire others to follow their hearts to bring medical care to a poor village in Africa, or to save a species of hummingbird threatened with extinction. Perhaps our example will inspire a teen who will one day become a Nobel Laureate.

Who knows where living your life fully will lead you and those you love? You won't know if you don't try.

We have been given a unique suite of gifts that makes each of us special and in turn makes our lives unique. We've been asked to use these gifts to their fullest as an expression of gratitude and love. We're being asked to live in joy, to live in love, to live with energy and creativity, to step out of our comfort zones and take a chance on ourselves to make our lives full, complete, and wonderfully extraordinary.

When we do that, when we use our gifts to better ourselves and the world, to live full and joyous lives, our souls rejoice, and so does the spiritual world. It is as if we are sending a huge "thank you" out to the universe. With our lives we are saying: I love what I have and I am using my gifts to their fullest, in love, in joy, and in beauty. Thank you!

We each have everything inside of us or at our disposal to live loving, beauty-filled, glorious, full lives. The only thing really standing in our way is ourselves. Our own preconceived ideas and fears limit us. Many of us fall into the trap of thinking "small," of not believing that we have the capacity to live the full lives that our hearts crave. Instead, we might settle for a life on autopilot, one that is much less fulfilling than our hearts long for us to live. Our ideas of what life *should* be like, how things *should* work out, how people *should* be — these all limit us and keep us from living our lives to their fullest.

We learn these "shoulds" from our families, our childhood friends, the schools we attend, religious groups, political parties, and from society in general. They don't intend to teach us to limit our thinking about what we can do with our lives. After all, they endured the same training themselves. But it can be frightening or difficult to break free of this programmed way of thinking, to step into our own amazing abilities, and to live the lives we were each given.

Nelson Mandela didn't let "should" thinking stand in the way of bringing his vision into reality. He didn't allow *what came before* to limit his grand idea for the way things could be. Instead, he allowed his thinking to expand into a South Africa the likes of which never existed before. He lived his life fully, and in doing so made life better for many other people, both in his country and around the world.

You don't have to be another Nelson Mandela or a global force for change, but you could try to be a Nelson Mandela for yourself. Set free your own thinking and limiting beliefs. See what kind of vision you can generate for your own life. Follow your heart and see where it leads. It may just bring you to wondrous things!

By living and loving ourselves and our lives fully, we show our love and gratitude to Spirit for this very special and sacred gift. We need to look within our own minds and hearts to find our personal roadmaps to the full and enriching lives we are meant to live. Each of our roadmaps will be different, but each is beautiful in its own way.

Living our lives intentionally and fully won't solve every problem on its own. We may have to do some work: learn new ways of listening and communicating, learn to let go of the power of our own egos, learn to live more fully in the present moment, to really be present in our relationships, and learn that everyone is different and on a different path through life.

MY THOUGHTS

Whether you believe that this is our only life or that we live multiple lives, the truth is that the life you are living right now is the only chance you have to live *as you*.

The you of this life has a unique set of talents, thoughts, feelings, strengths, weaknesses, ideas, and passions. These are your gifts, your tools for living a full and amazing life, right now.

Do you feel as though you are living your life fully?

Let's assume for a moment that reincarnation is real. Some might think this allows us to take a "pass" on this life, that we have an opportunity to do everything again. Nope. Even if reincarnation is real, when you come back you would be a different person with a different body, different personality, different strengths, different passions, another set of talents, and different potential. You will have lost the opportunity to make the most of the life you're in now.

This life is the only opportunity we each have to live fully as the person we are now. This is it.

What are we waiting for?

I faced this message head-on while lying in that hospital bed after my accident. Finally understanding this message — that this life was the one shot I had at living as ME — helped me develop a determination to make changes. I realized that I had allowed myself to coast up until then. I let society and well-meaning family and friends dictate to me the kind of life I should live. The hard part came in admitting to myself that it wasn't the life I wanted.

Lying in that hospital bed gave me the opportunity to internalize just how close I'd come to losing everything. There is nothing like spending two weeks in a broken body, totally dependent on others, to bring reality into sharp focus. The fact that I came close to squandering my chance to live a full, rewarding life really hit me hard. I had always wanted to have a creative life as an artist and writer, and in a heartbeat that opportunity was nearly plucked from my hands. I finally understood to my core that this life could be over, or turned inside out, in a split second.

Fortunately, I came away from this experience with the understanding that I wanted to live well, fully, and creatively now, whether that fit in with society's norms or not. I wanted to live the best life I possibly could given who I was, and I didn't want to spend another minute doing anything that felt wrong to me. This *now* is the only time I have to make my life the best it can be.

When we're young children, we tend to live life simply as we are. We live from an intuitive or heart-centered space, just being the people that we are at our cores. But as we grow, oftentimes our parents and society begin to influence us away from our true selves. In his book *The Four Agreements*, don Miguel Ruiz calls this process "domestication." Not knowing any better, we allow other people to influence the image we have of ourselves and what we want for our lives.

Some of us who are very strong, independent, or strongly in tune with our inner selves resist this process to a degree and have an easier time living life on our own terms. Many people aren't strong enough to resist, though, and go through years of living falsely before realizing who they really are in their hearts. Sadly, some people never understand, and remain unhappy inside but never knowing why.

The key is to find a path that allows us to live and work in this society, but that doesn't quash who we are inside. Embracing a more balanced approach to life is healthier and probably more fulfilling.

What I learned from my Guide is that God doesn't want us to live in a hollow way. Our spiritual source wants the best for us, wants us to be joyful and happy, and wants us to experience amazing things here in this life. Our blueprint for that is wrapped up in our personalities and our hearts, so the only way we can live a life in harmony with Spirit is to unroll that blueprint and start living from it.

Living life fully, loving who we are, and using the gifts that we've been given, is living in a state of gratitude and appreciation to our spiritual source. Living this way is truly living in love and grace.

What Does "Living Fully" Mean?

In my view, living fully means loving yourself — strengths and weaknesses both — and then committing to staying as much in alignment as possible with who you are. This is your gift of gratitude and love back to God. You are saying, "I see what I am. I love who I am. I am grateful for the gift of life you have given me, and I am going to live that life as fully as possible as a way to show my gratitude and love."

Living fully doesn't necessarily mean chucking all that you own and joining a convent or an ashram, becoming a circus performer, or busking on the streets. You don't have to live solely in-the-moment, either. It's OK and wise to plan for a future, to raise your kids wisely, to have some comforts and conveniences, and to think long-term. Just try as much as you can to live in alignment with your core self.

Learn to live your truth.

If in your heart you love dancing, you don't necessarily have to leave your job to try to become a professional dancer. Perhaps switching up your hobbies to include some folk dancing lessons in your free time might be enough. It makes sense to find and keep a job or career that aligns with who you are or what you want from life. The reality is that we all have bills to pay. But it doesn't need to become your entire life; you can do other things that you love outside of work, to keep your life interesting and fulfilling.

If animals tug at your heartstrings, you might want to change your career to something more in-alignment with that love. But it also might be just as enjoyable for you to volunteer with animal rescue groups, or to foster pets that need homes.

Living fully also means being truly mentally and emotionally present, as much as possible, for those people you most care about, including yourself. For example, when you're helping your son with his homework, pay full attention to him and try not to let your mind wander to the many other things you could be doing. Listen to him. Be there for him. Encourage. Help him patiently and lovingly.

Living fully doesn't necessarily mean taking daredevil risks either. Sure, if your heart is that of a rock climber, then spend time pursuing that love, safely. But living fully doesn't mean that you must put your life in danger or be an extreme athlete. Simply live as closely as possible to what's in your heart and you'll be on the right path.

If you have a dream or a goal, living fully means figuring out if you really want to do it or if it's even remotely feasible. It may be that something related to your goal will fulfill your dream just as nicely. For example, a young girl might have a dream of playing professional American football. The reality is that as a girl, being out on the field as a player is likely not in the cards for her, but being a television sportscaster covering professional football games is a distinct possibility. Another option for her might be to join a women's football squad. It might not be at a professional level but could still satisfy her dream.

If you choose to go forward with making your dream into a goal, figure out the steps you need to make that dream a reality then start off by tackling the first one.

Fear

Another reason many of us don't live our fullest lives, or live what comes from the heart, is fear. Sometimes we allow fears to make our decisions for us. I know — I've been there.

We allow fears of what others might think dictate the jobs we choose, the people we marry, or the places we live. We allow fear of failure to keep us from returning to school to finish our degree, or from writing that book we've been toying with for years. We're afraid of not having enough money or success and we choose careers that don't mesh with our true heart desires. Sometimes we're even afraid of succeeding. Fear is an insidious and crazy thing, isn't it?

Fear is a form of negative energy that sends ripples outward from us into the world. If we feel afraid, we'll act afraid and send that message out through words and actions.

We might allow the fear of death to hogtie us and prevent us from truly living. We avoid thinking about death. We play it safe even when we know we want to take a calculated risk in a career, in love, or with an adventure, in a hobby, etc. We don't take that overseas vacation because we're afraid the plane will crash. Or we spend a lot of mental energy in angst about dying, energy that might be better spent doing something that will help us reach a goal.

Unfounded fears prevent us from truly enjoying the here and now of living this life.

But examining our fears and respecting the message they are trying to tell us can be useful. We don't have to give in to the fear, but we can sure learn from it. Here's an example: at one point in my life I endured abusive behavior from someone I loved and trusted. As a result of living with this volatile energy, I became very in-tune with the moods and body language of the people around me. Even now, I run into people occasionally whose presence causes a shiver of fear to run up and down my spine. Instead of simply reacting to it by acting out, though, I give a little thought as to why I'm feeling that fear. Most of the time that I feel this fear, I realize that the person in question is behaving or communicating in a way that reminds me of the abusive behavior I endured earlier. It's a warning flag: something about this person may not be safe. If that happens, I can choose to simply and cautiously move along.

Fear can help us if we use it wisely, but most of us allow unfounded fears to run our lives. If this happens to me, I usually bring my intuition, heart, and head into the game. I first calm down with physical exercise or meditation. Next I allow my intuition, heart, and mind to really speak to me. What am I *really* feeling beneath the fear? Does this situation bring to mind something else that happened in the past? Is there something about this situation that my conscious self is missing but my subconscious recognizes? What can I do to mitigate any potential negative outcomes?

I then put into place any safety mechanisms that will help allay my fear, then step out onto the path my heart intends for me.

COMING TO TERMS WITH DEATH

Knowing without a doubt I will die, and that somehow part of "me" survives death has been the most freeing knowledge to come out of this whole experience. No, I'm not doing daredevil things in an effort to taunt the Grim Reaper, but I am now more likely to take calculated risks. By calculated I mean that I think about the pros and cons, consider the possible outcomes, and plan out what types of things I need to do or keep in mind with whatever I'm considering. Then I check in with my intuition and heart, and make the decision.

If the possible outcomes are pretty bleak (such as me trying out for a professional football team, or walking alone at night through the toughest big-city neighborhood), or my heart says "no," then I won't do it. If my heart says yes and I don't see too many downsides of a "yes" decision, I'll go for it. I might plan out some ways to deal with any potential challenges, but I'll go ahead and step out onto the new path.

What's the worst that could happen if I go for it? Will I die? Probably not. But even if I do, death isn't all that bad. That may sound flippant, but it's how I approach things these days.

Here's an example from my own life. After my accident, I had a lot of time to understand just how much I needed time off my job to heal and explore new paths.

I thought about options. For medical reasons, I still couldn't work more than half time, so that ruled out most jobs. More importantly, I knew that in my heart, I wanted to give my painting and writing a chance to become a career.

I thought about the possible downsides of trying to make a go of it. I couldn't come up with too many. Financially I was in good enough shape to take a decent amount of time off if I needed to. My sisters and friends supported me in my desire for a creative life. My artistic, marketing, and communication skills were finally at the point where I thought I could make a go of it. And I'd started a successful business before so I knew what was involved. I had experience.

The downside? The only one I could think of is that some people might think I was crazy. But I can't live my life worried about what other people are going to think. I knew I needed to listen to my instincts and my heart and make my own decision.

As of this writing (winter, 2014), it's too soon to tell if my new career path is a complete success, although I am seeing some good signs in new customers, sales, and art show invitations. I do feel more in line with my spiritual source, my stress levels are much lower, and I feel more "me" than I have ever felt before. I'm also having fun, I'm forging a strong connection with my spirituality, and I feel in my heart that I have made the right decision for me.

Since I know that I will die someday, the last thing in the world I wanted was to be on my deathbed wishing I hadn't been too afraid to make a go of a creative career.

So I'm doing it.

OTHER PEOPLE

These were decisions I made for myself as a fully capable, independent adult. But on a spiritual level, we really don't have the right to unduly influence other people's decisions. Each person is on his or her own path in this life and there is no way that we can know what that path is for someone else. Trying to control or influence the decisions of other adults is at best disrespectful and at worst manipulative.

Do you like being told what to do or how to live your life? No? I know that I don't. Knowing how I feel about being manipulated or controlled makes me very conscious of how my words and actions might unduly influence other people.

We are responsible for caring for our kids or other dependents, yes, teaching them to make good decisions and to take care of themselves so they can become capable, independent adults. But it's not our responsibility to make all of their decisions for them or force them on a path that isn't in alignment with their core selves. They have their own personalities, strengths, inspiration, creativity, and gifts that we may not fully understand or even know about. Our kids need to learn to grow into responsible adults and to make heart-based decisions backed by their own feeling and thinking. We can help them do that, and that's why we're here.

We're guides and mentors, not drill sergeants. We want the best for our kids but we often don't know what that really means for them over the course of their lives. They do, though, through their own connection to their spiritual source. Like us, our kids have that inner knowledge to provide them a map to live their best lives. Our job is to help them access this map by teaching them to respect what is in their hearts and how to live a fully functioning life.

Can you imagine Giovanni di Pietro di Bernardone, an Italian nobleman's son in medieval Italy, blindly following his father's example and becoming a silk merchant? Instead, he followed the calling in his heart, turned his life toward his Creator, and became the man we know as St. Francis of Assisi, a powerful force for love and light.

Practice Living Fully

Each person has his or her own idea of what living a full life means. Again, I can't tell you what this would be for you, but I'll give you some examples of things that help me to live my life more fully.

- *Are you being held back by fears?* What are you afraid of? Are you concerned about what others might think of you? Do you make decisions based on what other people want for your life?
- *Have you let fear make decisions for you in the past?* Think or journal about some of those fear-based decisions. Is there a common theme that you can work on? Maybe fear of failure, or fear of what others might think?
- *If you have some fears, think about the worst that could happen if they were to come true.* Is there any way to mitigate or lessen the impact of some of these potential negative outcomes? What is the real likelihood of this fear actually happening?
- *Are you either openly or subtly trying to control how others live their lives?* It's OK if you are — most of us do — after all, we're only human. Think about ways you can back off and allow them to control their own future. If the person you're trying to influence is your child, are there ways you can let her have a little more autonomy in her own life while still making sure she's safe and cared for?
- *Try the Miracle Exercise: if you had no fears and all of your needs were taken care of, what would your life look like?* How would it be different from your current life? What would you do? Where would you live? Take some time to really think about it or write about it if you'd like. Then think about ways you can take steps to make some of these things reality. For example, if your dream life involves playing guitar, can you start taking lessons now?

CHAPTER 17
Gratitude

———⚯———

LIVE AND FEEL YOUR GRATITUDE *every day.*
Everything in our world is a gift. Gratitude for the things we have and experience is our way of demonstrating love to our spiritual source for these gifts. We've been asked to feel and express gratitude for both the small and big things, and to show our gratitude to others for what they bring to our lives.

FULL MESSAGE

In my little slice of Heaven, the love of Spirit filtered through everything. There was nowhere that was separate from that loving energy. When I walked through the groves of trees and looked up to see pearly sunlight filtering through branches, I felt God's love there, showering down on me from above. Beams of sunlight carried love. Breezes brought the Divine presence to embrace all parts of the landscape. I somehow felt everything around me singing with joy at this loving connection to Spirit.

Even toward the end of my stay there, when I protested going back to my life, I still felt the love of God and my Guide warming my being. The landscape still reverberated with love. And that's when my Guide gave me one more insight. She allowed me to see and fully experience how those in Heaven show love back to God.

That joyful "song" or hum that I sensed from everything around me? That was joy-filled gratitude in its most pure form.

Every being in Heaven sent feeling-waves of deep gratitude back to Spirit. The gratitude was part of the flow of loving energy; it was the way that spiritual beings gave love back to God. I can't describe how this *felt*, really. While my Guide immersed me in this flow of love and gratitude so I could experience it myself, I can't describe what it felt like other than mystical and hypnotic, but natural and liberating at the same time.

Being *that* connected to Spirit through love and gratitude may seem overwhelming or stifling to us, but to spiritual beings, it's simply a part of existence, like breathing is to us. Those beings have individuality, but at the same time they exist in a state of constant love and gratitude in concert with the Divine.

In Heaven, gratitude and love are two sides of the same coin. My Guide showed me that the same is true here, too. Gratitude is a form of deep love and appreciation. It's more than just lip-service or a recitation of memorized words — it really is the deep feelings in our bodies and souls that go along with the grateful words we might choose to express. When we allow ourselves to *deeply feel* gratitude in the core of our beings, and then express it verbally, we truly feel love and appreciation for what we *do* have.

If you express appreciation to another person and allow yourself to *really feel it* internally, the recipient will likely feel your sentiment is genuine and heart-felt. He or she will truly sense the love and appreciation that you feel in that moment.

Gratitude does come back to help us, too. True gratitude cleanses the heart and the soul. It makes us feel good. Feeling gratitude deeply bathes us in that warmth of love. How might we feel after we allow deep appreciation to wash through our hearts? We may feel more at peace and more connected to the people around us (or to God, or nature). We might feel relief, or perhaps we will cry and be overcome with joy.

Gratitude is also our way of demonstrating our love and appreciation back to the Divine for what we have. We might verbally say a prayer of gratitude or "thank you" aloud, but nothing makes a bigger impact spiritually than allowing ourselves to truly *feel* that gratitude in our hearts.

To feel love and appreciation is gratitude's purest and deepest form of expression. The power of those feelings emanate from you, much more than words alone. Love transcends all — physical and spiritual.

We can also choose to *live* our gratitude daily. Feeling it is wonderful, but transforming that feeling into some positive action is even more powerful. Allowing that gratitude to propel us to do good works in service to others is another tangible expression of love.

Some might call this concept "paying it forward." Others appreciate it when we allow positive actions to follow our feelings of gratitude, so try to be of service and let that transform your life as well as the lives you touch. This type of loving service creates a wave of positive energy and actions that moves out from us and then affects others.

Gratitude Is Not a Tool

My Guide took exception to a notion popular in some New Age spiritual arenas that gratitude is a way of *getting more* rather than what it truly is: feeling and giving love and appreciation. The New Age view promotes the idea that lip-service "gratitude" is a means for us to get more material goods, more money, more romance, more adoration, or more friends. In other words, it's some kind of back-door way of forcing God to give us something we don't have but really want.

For example, let's say you want a new sports car but can't afford one at the moment. This modern view of gratitude says to verbally thank God for the car well before it's even a possibility for you to acquire. The idea is that pretending that you already have the car by thanking Spirit for it will somehow make the Spirit bring the car into your life. You don't even need to *feel* gratitude for the car you don't have, you simply have to thank Spirit for it and it will come to you.

You are, in effect, trying to coerce the spiritual powers-that-be into sending you the car.

You may indeed get the car by using some of these techniques (asking, visualizing, thinking from the end), but my Guide asks that you don't use gratitude; feel it with a loving heart and soul. Don't worry so much about that car you don't have. *Feel* gratitude for what you do have, right now, in this moment. Keep practicing that feeling of gratitude as much as you can.

My Guide explained that the manipulative, unfeeling sort of gratitude I describe above is not loving, grateful, or spiritual. She was also concerned that people weren't truly *understanding* what gratitude really is.

At heart, gratitude is not self-centered. True gratitude is a deep feeling of love and appreciation for what we *do* have, for what we have been given, and for what we experience every day of our lives no matter how small or insignificant. *The purpose of gratitude is not to get more stuff. Its sole purpose is to show love and appreciation.*

That's it. It all comes back to love.

It Does Come Back

In Chapter 9, I wrote about how what we project outward, we eventually get back in some way. This works for the love that is gratitude too.

While we might actually *get* more coming back into our own lives when we truly *feel* that love and appreciation of gratitude, we're asked not to allow the pursuit of material goods to be the sole reason we allow ourselves to feel grateful. Material goods are fleeting at best. Our garbage dumps are filled with all of the things we simply had to have just a few years ago.

But spiritual love outlasts material goods. A strong, loving relationship on Earth can last a human lifetime and weather countless storms. Allowing ourselves to feel and express love and appreciation to others can enhance these relationships and thus bring us more of what many of us truly desire — deep connectedness and closeness to others.

Doesn't a truly wonderful, caring relationship trump the latest cell phone?

What good are material things if we are miserably alone in our homes all day? Yes, those material things can be fun and it's perfectly fine to experience them if we desire, but they are limited in what they can do for us. Alone, they likely won't help us forge the connections to others that we crave.

A television won't give you a shoulder to cry on when your father dies. A computer won't share your joy at the birth of your daughter or son. And the latest electronic gadget won't comfort you or give you strength through a terrifying medical diagnosis. Only love from another human and love from your spiritual source can do that. And to build both of those connections, to make them truly strong, you will need to feel and express your gratitude.

Gratitude really does strengthen these heart-centered bonds. It reinforces them and helps them grow. Gratitude brings everything we love and appreciate, closer to our hearts. It creates for them a safe, soft, warm place in our souls, and it makes us feel good too. If we're expressing gratitude to other people, it makes them feel good as well. It may help them open up and want to forge a closer connection to us because they feel appreciated. But this happens only if the love and appreciation are genuine. Remember that almost everyone, including Spirit, can sense when your gratitude is genuine and heartfelt.

Love and Gratitude for Ourselves

Everything around us has loving energy at its core. And gratitude strengthens love.

Take a moment to let that sink in; see if you can tease out the connection. Gratitude helps to strengthen the good in the world around us. It's an amplifier to love.

When we feel grateful, keeping our minds and hearts in that feeling for as long as we can is like a prayer or meditation. It feels good and *is* good for us. It calms our spirits. It can soothe our fears and anxieties. It helps exercise and grow our capacity for love.

Channel some of your gratitude back to yourself too. After all, you deserve love just as much as anyone else! Be grateful to yourself for working on achieving or maintaining a healthy body, mind, and spirit. Be grateful to yourself for having the persistence to achieve a goal or to emotionally support a friend in need. Find ways every day to feel gratitude towards *you*.

Why?

This kind of self-appreciation shows Spirit that you love this amazing creation that is *you*. It also sends some of that positive energy back in to your life. Appreciate the health that you do have, even if you feel ill. Appreciate the strength that you have, your wit, your sense of humor, whatever uniqueness that is yours. All of it. Remember that your gratitude and appreciation will strengthen anything you direct it towards, including your own abilities and talents.

Love and appreciate your body, every glorious inch of it. Be grateful for the marvel that it is: how thousands, millions, or billions of components work together seamlessly to make up you.

Appreciate your mind and emotions — both their whole and broken parts.

Appreciate your spiritual center — for it is the place where you most strongly feel the connection to Spirit.

Gratitude for Tough Times

This next concept may seem a little counter-intuitive. My Guide suggested that we try to feel some level of gratitude for the negatives in our lives as well as the positives. This can be difficult, especially if the negatives involve the illness or death of someone we love or some other terrible misfortune in our lives. But those negatives are a part of living. The negatives can teach us a lot about life, the world, spirituality, and ourselves.

Try to pull some kernel of learning or gratitude out of each negative event. Are you closer to your father because of his illness? Is your heart more open to love now that you have experienced the death of someone you cherished? Did a terrible accident allow you to reorganize your life in a positive direction? Did you learn a valuable lesson as a result of a negative interaction with a coworker?

See if you can find something to be grateful for in challenging situations. Direct some loving thoughts toward them, allowing time for deeper meaning or understanding to come forth. This might be one way to help you uncover the gift hidden inside those tough times.

While we don't want to experience difficulties, it's best to try not to hate or fear them. How we handle the experience, and what we take away from it is often more important than the event itself.

Send love and appreciation to all of the events in your life, whether easy or difficult. The difficulties make us grow stronger and deeper in faith, the easy times are gifts to enjoy and savor.

My Guide passed this on to me to demonstrate the effects that difficulties may have on our lives:

> *"Do you notice that oftentimes, downstream of a rapids or a waterfall the river runs deeper and its surface is calmer? That is how events in our lives can affect us if we allow them that space. After a rough spot, we are often deeper in spirit and have a calmer surface, just like that river."*

My Thoughts

In this era of New Age gurus, many of us seem to have acquired a notion that the only reason to be grateful is to get more. It's become a way for us to manipulate the universe into getting what we want or feel that we deserve. Nothing could be further from the truth.

If spiritual beings could be angry, my Guide was angry over how we viewed gratitude.

She laid her distress and sadness on me with all of the force of raw emotion. Her disappointment and sadness nearly overwhelmed me. I couldn't remain standing through the force of her sadness. I fell to my knees and wept.

After I recovered, she went on to explain that gratitude is really quite simple: it is a feeling that we allow to build in our hearts, a feeling made of love and appreciation for someone or something. Then we vocalize this feeling into words such as "thank you."

The feeling should come first, if possible. Saying the words without feeling the underlying emotions is not as powerful, spiritually-speaking.

It's simple, although it might not be easy:

1. Focus on the love and appreciation you feel for the things in your life.
2. Express your gratitude.
3. Don't expect to "get" anything in return.

Gratitude isn't a trade agreement — I say "Thank you, God" and God gives me a new car in return. Nope. Feel and express your sincere gratitude and leave it at that.

You may very well get something back in return for feeling grateful. More things may just come into your life. If you are sincerely grateful to your spouse for helping out with the kids, and then express it, you might just get a hug, or a kiss, or even more help with the kids. If you feel and express gratitude to your employees for working on a weekend to meet a deadline, they may be more willing to help you out in similar situations in the future.

The moral of the story is: don't be grateful for the sole purpose of getting more. Gratitude is really about giving love back.

FEELING MY GRATITUDE

After my cycling accident, I was overwhelmed by the amount of love, support, and assistance people around me directed my way. Family and friends, yes, but complete strangers too. I was often overcome with emotion — how could people I didn't know be so loving and helpful to me? The emotion I felt was centered in my heart area, and it was often so strong that it brought tears to my eyes. Yet it felt good somehow, and right. I could feel the love that ran from the giver to me. There were times when I would lie in my hospital bed for hours, just allowing this feeling-state of loving bliss to continually wash through me.

It took me a while to really understand that what I was feeling was the raw emotion of gratitude. The love and appreciation that I felt seemed *large* somehow. It felt as if a small sun was in my heart, warming me from inside. Love, amazement, appreciation, and joy formed the core of this small sun of gratitude. I felt humbled that so many people were giving so much to me, without expecting anything in return.

Now, months later, when I am grateful for less momentous things, I still feel a beautiful sun of love, but it seems smaller in scale. It shines brightly, but not as brightly or intensely as in those first few months after my accident. The feeling is still there in my heart but it doesn't overwhelm me too often. I might revel in it but I can still pay attention to life and whatever I am doing. Today's gratitude is more often like a little candle flame or a fireplace in my heart rather than a star.

It took being overwhelmed by that big sense of gratitude, though, in order for me to understand how it felt inside in its purest form. I'd never really felt it *that* deeply before, to my soul level. During those initial months when the feeling was so strong in my body, I learned that this feeling is the first and most important part of gratitude. The feeling is really a form of deep love, and Spirit feels your love whether you put verbal words to it or not.

For those of us who are not used to truly *feeling* gratitude in our bodies, doing so might take a little time. Below is a practice I use on myself. It might help you too. Take some time out of your day and try to locate that feeling of gratitude in your own body with the following contemplation:

Sit alone in a quiet place where you are safe (not operating machinery). Turn off your cell phone and make sure you have no distractions.

Start by trying to feel gratitude for something really big in your life — perhaps for the birth of a child, for the love of a spouse or partner, or for someone saving your life. What comes to mind?

Now close your eyes, and contemplate it.
Think about the enormity of the gift that was given to you. Think about the positive impact it has had, or will have, on your life. Think about all it took for everything to fall into place in order for this event to happen. Allow these thoughts to really hit home. Savor them, let them reverberate in your heart.

Did anyone make a sacrifice or put something on the line for you when it wasn't required? Why did they do it? Did they have to do it? Or was it simply an act of love and compassion? Think about that, too.

After a few minutes of contemplating the event or the people, do a mental scan of your body. Are you starting to feel something? Are you choked up, with tears in your eyes? Does your heart area feel warm, light, or energized? Are you smiling?

No one is watching, so it's OK to allow any emotions to come out. You have nothing to apologize for. If you want to cry, cry.

If you are feeling some emotion in your body, sit with it for a few minutes and allow the impact of those feelings to wash through you. Revel in that sense of gratitude.

I do this exercise several times a week. If you're new to feeling gratitude, this exercise might help increase your ability to feel it when done regularly. At some point, your ability to feel grateful may become second nature and you can ease off this exercise.

The more you feel your gratitude for the bigger things, the easier it will be to feel grateful for smaller, less momentous events, such as the beauty of a sunrise or the sweet scent of a beautiful rose.

Expressing Gratitude

Once you're comfortable with feeling your gratitude, it's time to start expressing it verbally it to both Spirit and the people in your life.

First, feel the grateful feeling. Next, say a heartfelt "thank you" or "I appreciate you for _____" aloud.

Smile. That's it.

Not too difficult, is it?

Practice Gratitude

Below are just a few ideas for making gratitude a daily feeling and practice[31]. Pick one that feels right and start with that, or come up with your own ways of feeling and expressing your gratitude:

- *Begin a gratitude journal.* Some people feel more of a connection to Spirit when they write, so if that's you, grab a notebook and write down five things that you're grateful for each day. Feel free to spread them out over different areas of your life, or let them be clustered around one event. Anything you're grateful for is OK. You might choose to separate your personal from your professional or business life — it's OK any way you choose. The notebook can be a beautiful one if you'd like, but it doesn't need to be. Anything that you feel comfortable writing in will do. Make sure that you try to feel the gratitude while you are writing. Words not backed by the feeling don't mean as much spiritually. Perhaps you're feeling thankful that your kids gave

---

[31] Check out Amy Collette's book, *The Gratitude Connection,* for more exercises that will help you make gratitude a part of your daily life.

you an extra hug before they left for school this morning. Maybe your boss gave you a raise that you really need. Perhaps your best friend called you out of the blue to see how you're doing. Maybe your spouse sent you flowers today. It doesn't matter how big or small these things are. Feel the gratitude and write them down in your journal.

- *If you don't feel the desire to write things down, simply think about five things you're grateful for at the end of each day.* Again, feel the feeling, then verbalize your gratitude. Yes, aloud. Spirit can hear even if no one else can.
- *Feel gratitude and say "thank you" to as many people as you can during the day, and mean it.* Do it without expecting anything in return.
- *Find something to be grateful for in a difficult relationship in your life.* Spend some time contemplating the other person. Is there anything you have learned, or can learn, from interacting with him or her? Can you find something positive to take away from this difficult relationship? If so, be and feel grateful for what you've learned.
- *Find something to be grateful for in a tough situation.* Spend time thinking about it. Can you learn anything? Can you find something positive to take away from these tough times? Will you grow stronger as a result of having experienced this? If so, be and feel grateful for what you've learned or how you've changed.

PART THREE

Recovering

CHAPTER 18

Body and Mind

MY TRANSITION BACK TO LIFE was not an easy one. The memory of being in Heaven played through my mind almost non-stop for several days after surgery. I wanted to return, but at the same time I wondered if I'd simply gone off the deep end and invented it all in some strange, psychotic episode. I struggled with the reality of the experience and tried not to think of the implications of what I'd seen, felt, and learned.

ON SOME DEEPER LEVEL, AT the core of my being, I knew the experience was real. It seemed too logical and rational to have been hallucination. It made too much sense. Many years prior, I did hallucinate from prescription pain medication – that experience was crazy, nonsensical, and definitely not logical.

I've always had a very good intuitive sense — my "gut feelings" had often been on-target even when my mind was wrong. Over time I had learned to trust my intuition. In those days after surgery, my intuition screamed to me that my experience was real and that, in some strange way, it was even more real than my life on Earth.

At first I kept quiet about my otherworldly experience. I felt too scared of what people might think to divulge what I experienced. I envisioned being committed to a psychiatric hospital if I told my doctors about touring Heaven while in surgery.

The desire to go back to wherever I'd been haunted me, though. Several times during those first days I tried to make my case with Spirit to just take me back. Pleading that I didn't want to be here in the hospital, going through such physical and emotional pain, didn't work though. It seemed I was stuck in my body.

In The Hospital

Happily, my body was faring remarkably well. The surgeon had installed the titanium rods without any problems and within a day or two after the procedure, my incision looked remarkably good. A rigid but removable body cast allowed me to get up out of bed and move around without worrying about damaging my newly-reconstructed spine. My doctors required that I wear the cast whenever I wasn't flat on my back. I could only remove it for sleeping and briefly during a shower for the next six weeks, possibly up to twelve, depending on how quickly I healed. I didn't enjoy hearing "twelve weeks" so I made a pact with myself to do everything I could to heal quickly. Since the body cast was fabricated from a heavy-gauge plastic, it felt hot and restricting. But at least it would allow me to get up and walk around without feeling scared I would re-injure my back.

My friends told me I looked a bit like a valkyrie when it was on. I laughed at that, but inside, a part of me felt like Frankenstein's monster, too: sewn together, battered, worn, and walking with an unstable shuffle to my gait. But at least I was walking, and I felt very grateful that I wasn't learning how to use a wheelchair.

Pain plagued me, though. The post-surgical pain felt worse by far than anything I'd experienced, including childbirth. While my collarbone, ribs, and sternum miraculously didn't hurt, the pain in my back and neck more than made up for it. At least nine vertebrae sustained fractures or breaks, and some of them sported multiple fractures. The surgical incision in my lower back was extremely painful, as were the muscles under the incision, and even my spine itself.

For the first few days after surgery, I continued to take prescription opioids for the pain. But the side effects took their toll on me and by the third day after surgery, I wanted to be off pain meds. Since I was so sensitive to pain medications, the only thing left for me to take was acetaminophen. It wasn't as powerful, but it was enough to take the edge off and allow me to walk. It also didn't have any distressing mental and physical side effects.

An unexpected problem arose the day after surgery. My body began retaining fluids and started to swell. My legs and abdomen swelled to the point where they looked as if they would be better suited to an elephant than a person! The doctors told me that the swelling was the result of the anesthesia and the opioids, but I didn't care about the cause. I simply wanted it gone. I felt bloated and ugly, and I didn't want anyone I knew to see me in this state.

Even though I felt grateful to be walking, I struggled physically and mentally with the process of relearning to move. Just the small act of walking out to the nurses' station felt like climbing Mt. Everest. My legs felt heavy from the accumulating fluid and weak from trauma, pain medication, and surgery. The body cast and a neck brace made movement even more challenging, and my left arm was in a sling to protect my collarbone. I needed assistance to do almost everything: put on my body cast, get out of bed, go to the bathroom, shower, dress, walk, and even eat.

I had gone from fiercely independent to totally dependent in the blink of an eye. This abrupt change terrified me because I worried that I'd never regain my independence. I realized that I had no choice and finally let go. I simply allowed myself to depend on others because I needed help to heal. But I made a vow to myself that I do everything I could to be back on my feet in record time.

In the hospital, my morning routine started with a nursing assistant helping me into my body cast. It was an odd, stiff "clamshell" contraption with a loose hinge on one side. I didn't actually put it on as much as I rolled into it. Turning onto my right side allowed my helper to place one half of the open cast against my back. Then rolling backwards onto the bed forced my body back into the cast so that my helper could position it correctly and secure it. Only when it felt secure could I sit up vertically on the side of the bed.

It felt like plastic plated mail armor, stifling and restricting, but it did its job of holding my spine in the correct posture while allowing me to stand and walk.

With my body armor in place, on the second day after surgery the nurses gave me free rein to move about the room or out into the hallways, with a walker and an escort of course. In effect, I was relearning the fine art of putting weight on my legs, then moving them on command, and finally walking. I felt a lot of frustration at first. After all, just a few days ago I was capable of hiking, running, and cycling without a second thought. My body just worked. Now it didn't. I allowed myself to feel the frustration for a short time, but then a calmness washed through me. I somehow simply became aware that my healing was a process. A slow one, yes, but one that would happen better if I calmed down and simply cooperated. That didn't mean I never had another moment of frustration — I did many times during my healing process — but the frustration always fell away once I allowed myself to understand the sheer amount of healing my body needed to experience.

While re-learning how to walk, I developed a deep sense of compassion and empathy for others who were mobility-impaired or suffered brain trauma. My thoughts often turned to others who weren't as lucky as me: veterans who had lost limbs or suffered traumatic brain injuries, stroke victims, those paralyzed by accident or birth, and millions others like them. I had almost been there myself. If I had moved a little more at the scene of the crash, those slivers of bone in my spine would have put me in a wheelchair, permanently. My heart went out to those others who weren't as lucky. At least I could walk.

In those first few days after surgery, I used a walker initially but quickly graduated to a quad cane,[32] then later, to a standard cane. In

---

32 A quad cane is a cane that has a four feet rather than the single foot of a typical cane. Quad canes provide more stability than the standard cane.

order to go home, I knew that I needed to show I could walk and navigate a typical home environment.

Because I wanted to be in my own house as soon as possible, I walked the corridors as much as I could. I wanted my strength and endurance back *right now*. Being a patient didn't appeal to me at all. The sterile-looking environment, lack of sleep, frequent blood draws, and constant activity were at odds with my usual quiet and relaxed life. I liked being independent and enjoyed my alone time, but now all of that was gone. I knew that in time, I'd get those things back, but right now, being on my own again seemed a long way off.

My long-term prognosis still terrified me and now another fear joined that one: how my finances might fare as a result of the accident. It turned out that the driver had minimal insurance coverage and no assets. I would have little to no financial relief from her or her insurer. On top of that, my request for short-term disability benefits had been denied because the signup process, completed six weeks prior (or so I thought), actually had not been filed properly. The end result was that I had no short-term disability coverage through my employer. And since I had only recently been hired by the company, I didn't have the sick time built up that veteran employees did. I started to sink into an emotional black hole.

But a few small glimmers of hope did appear.

My broken clavicle, broken ribs, and bruised sternum still didn't hurt. They also didn't hurt through the entire process of healing over the next several months. This realization prompted me to wonder about that woman I met during my time close to death: my Guide. What really happened? Was I experiencing a placebo effect, or had my pain truly been taken away from me?

Soon after my surgery, one beautiful ray of light came into my life and gave me a tiny bit of hope that things might be OK in the end. A hospital chaplain came to visit me.

I have no idea why she came to my room. When the trauma staff initially admitted me to the ER, I indicated to them that I wasn't religious and didn't want to see a chaplain *at all* during my stay. So why she came to my room after surgery, I don't know. Whatever the reason for her visit, I'm glad she came.

She took a seat near the head of my bed, held my hand, and lent me her calming presence. In a bewildering rush of emotions, I found myself sobbing, telling her everything that happened to me during the crash and while I was in surgery. She listened intently but instead of telling me I was crazy, she quietly related that she had heard this type of thing before and knew that what I experienced was real. She explained that I had started to die, twice, and had two "Near-Death Experiences."[33] Somehow, her speaking that term made it all seem real rather than a figment of my imagination. There was a name for my experience, and it was considered real by many people.

What a relief!

Her interpretation was that the being I met in Heaven was an angel, and so was the woman (Ann) who kept me from getting up and running from the scene of the accident[34].

More important to me, though, is that she validated what I saw and felt. That turned out to be exactly what I needed.

The chaplain then bowed her head and prayed for my physical, mental, and emotional healing, then spent several more minutes with me in silent contemplation and prayer. Eventually she moved on to the next patient's room but that one short visit helped me to realize I wasn't crazy, that other people had experienced similar things, and gave me hope that I would be OK.

---

33 The first NDE occurred during the crash itself, when I felt my consciousness separate into two. The second was the longer one that occurred during surgery. Since I still wonder about what happened during the crash itself and don't fully consider my split consciousness a near-death experience, I only refer to only one NDE throughout this book.

34 She very well may be correct. After months of searching, the Boulder County, Colorado, District Attorney's office was unable to locate any evidence of Anne, other than my own account, and one police officer who reported seeing her. She is indeed a mystery.

About three days after surgery, the bottom once again dropped out of my emotional state. My older sister Mary and her husband Glenn arrived from Wisconsin to help me through the first part of my recovery process. I think my sister's presence allowed me to relax enough to have an almost complete emotional breakdown. I could cry, grieve, and feel whatever I needed to feel. For the next two days, I felt stuck in a terror that my world was ending.

In a way, it was.

I still didn't want to tell most people what had happened during surgery; definitely not my doctors, but I even kept it from most of my family and all of my friends at first. I was afraid they would think I was nuts!

But that Thursday after surgery I got up the courage to tell Mary about my experience. Her emotions still ran high from my accident, but she tried to listen and understand. I didn't go into a lot of detail, but I did tell her that I had almost died and wanted to go back to whatever that place was. I think it comforted her when I added that I wasn't being allowed to do that yet.

To my amazement, she listened even though she seemed frightened by my close call. But more importantly, she didn't think I was crazy. I also worked up the courage to tell my younger sister, Jennifer, a little about my experience and she too didn't think I was crazy.

Sharing the experience with my sisters helped to legitimize it for me. But then something else happened. Once I openly began talking about it with them, I realized the weight and enormity of the agreement I'd made with my Guide.

My contract with Spirit suddenly became all too real. I had a job to do.

I remembered what I'd been taught, remembered that I had a task to do, but a few details remained fuzzy. While that felt frustrating at first, I thought that if Spirit had given me a job then surely He would help me remember the few things still locked away in my brain.

I decided to use a tactic that worked in other areas of my life to help me remember: I talked. I hoped that by telling some of my close friends about my experience, I might remember the remaining details. I began by speaking with a few open-hearted friends over the phone, and they also turned out to be very receptive and encouraging.

A few days later, I finally told Angela, the woman who spent time with me before the surgery, and my friend Don. Both had come to visit me at the same time so I decided just to tell them what happened while they were in the room. I'm pretty good at reading facial expressions and feared what I might see. Again, both were receptive and didn't tell me I was crazy. Don reinforced the idea that I would remember the rest of the details when it was time.

With each telling, the experience became more legitimate in my mind and I realized that I wasn't crazy.

Through telling my story, I came to understand the reality of what I'd experienced, the enormity of what I was taught, and the depth of spiritual peace and love I'd encountered. I became more peace-filled, patient, and loving, too. Anxiety and terror melted away. My new Boss and my new job seemed pretty cool. Spirit expected a lot from me, but He also knew I could deliver. He trusted me, as did my Guide in Heaven.

A peaceful knowing that things were unfolding as they should washed through me. Some days might be rough, but I knew that all would be OK as long as I continued to walk in light and love. I lost any anger or bitterness about the accident and I still harbor none toward the driver. I think that amazed me and my family more than anything — that I was able to let go of being angry and just focus on the job that was coming.

The first task in my new job was to heal.

I decided to start incorporating what I'd learned from my Guide into my life. I treated my body as the gift it was: I fed it only healthy foods, treated it with love and respect, exercised it, all to help it be as healthy as possible. For me that meant completely avoiding my allergens of dairy, peanuts, legumes, most grains, and all processed food. I was determined to eat only whole, healthy foods in order to give my body the fuel it needed to repair itself.

My healing progressed but was slowed down by a hospital-acquired infection called *C. difficile*. I caught it sometime that first week in the hospital but didn't become symptomatic until four days post-surgery. *C. difficile* is a nasty intestinal bacteria that causes fever, nausea, and severe diarrhea. It's been known to cause death, too. For several days I battled the worst bacterial infection of my life, and many times I thought for sure I wouldn't make it through alive. A fever of 103 degrees Fahrenheit, delirium, and severe intestinal "distress" kept me in the hospital a full five days longer than I should have been.

My continuing thought, a stab at humor in my still-foggy state, was that I survived being run over by a truck, a surgery to reconstruct my back, and a trip to Heaven, only to be killed by a bacteria that no one could see without a microscope. I'm grateful that turned out to be an unfounded fear.

After a full two weeks in ICU and acute care, and dosed with enough antibiotics to kill an elephant, I had recovered enough to leave the hospital. I was discharged to a skilled nursing facility (SNF) for further rehabilitation because my case manager didn't feel comfortable sending me home right away. She suggested additional rehabilitation at the SNF.

I spent one grueling night there. It turned out that it was a nursing home and not a physical rehabilitation center as I thought, and definitely not the place for me to heal. Being there deflated my spirits. The other residents were very elderly, frail, and in extremely poor health. I had the sense that most seemed to be there waiting for death. Definitely not the environment I wanted for my healing![35]

I was transported to the SNF in the middle of the night and left on my own in an unused wing of the facility. I had not eaten at the hospital,

---

35 I realize that not all skilled nursing facilities are as dark and depressing as this one was. I felt sadness that we as a culture shut our elders away in places such as this to wait out the remainder of their lives. I understand we have many reasons for our elders' presence in nursing facilities, but in my opinion, we need to take a long, hard look at all of them. Are they loving and compassionately caring for the people entrusted to them? Are the residents safe? Are they getting excellent care? Are their emotional and spiritual needs being met? From my stay of just one night, I'm sure we can do much better than what I experienced.

and the SNF didn't offer me food either because the kitchen was closed. The bed they gave me was a temporary air bed that deflated in the middle of the night and I couldn't figure out how to fix it. I called for the nurse but it was almost an hour before one appeared. When a nurse finally did arrive, she couldn't fix the problem and after a couple more hours, I finally gave up and decided sleep wasn't in the cards.

In the morning, "breakfast" came and it consisted of some of the most horrid-looking food I could imagine. On top of that, I was allergic to almost all of it. While the nursing staff had noted my food allergies the previous night, it turned out that the kitchen had no way to accommodate them. They had nothing that I could safely eat even though when my family had interviewed the SNF admittance staff prior to my visit, they said that my food allergies weren't a problem. It turned out that if I were to stay here, my family would have to bring me all of my own food.

I was desperate to leave and return home.

The physical therapy staff evaluated me later that morning. They realized that I was actually too advanced in my mobility and recovery to be admitted to *any* skilled nursing facility. In their opinion, the most appropriate place for me was at home, with in-home physical therapy. Hallelujah! That was just what I needed to hear. Staff discharged me later that day.

My sister, brother-in-law, niece, and friend Angela helped me make the journey home. Finally! We had a bit of a struggle finding an appropriate vehicle to transport me in my body cast and neck brace, but it turned out that Angela's SUV worked nicely. So on a sunny afternoon two weeks after I left on my bike ride, I finally came home.

I felt so ecstatic to be in my own place again that I almost floated up my entry stairs!

My strength returned more rapidly now that I was home and eating only healthy foods, getting sunshine and fresh air, and sleeping as much as I wanted. Sleeping 10-12 hours a day became normal for me. For most of my life I usually slept only six or seven hours per night, so I felt a bit lazy sleeping for 10 or more hours a day. But I didn't struggle against my body's wisdom. I slept as much as my body required.

My sisters and a friend took turns staying with me for the next five weeks, helping me around the house, to take care of myself, and to relearn how to do previously simple tasks like cooking or laundry. Their loving care was a huge comfort to me during this time. Besides being a physical help, their presence allowed me to relax spiritually into what I had seen in my near-death experience.

BODY

When the accident first happened and I realized the extent of my injuries, I assumed that my physical healing would be much easier and quicker than my emotional healing. I've always healed quickly. And while I'd never broken a single bone before this, I had no indication that this time would be any different.

How wrong I was!

The first six weeks were a nightmare in many ways. My body remained confined in both the torso and hard neck braces. Maneuvering while wearing these devices was a chore at best. They were rigid, hot, uncomfortable, and restricting. They did their job of preventing me from moving my spine, though. Most of our everyday activities involve some kind of spinal movement: washing laundry, loading the dishwasher, getting in and out of bed, walking, getting food out of the refrigerator. In the past, I did all of these without thinking about how much my spine twisted and bent. With the hard tortoiseshell-like brace, though, I became acutely aware of how much my spine used to move during a day. Now the only place my body would bend was at my hips and knees. Dropping something on the floor meant I would have to bend down onto my knees to pick it up, or ask one of my sisters to get it for me.

Help eventually arrived in the form of an in-home physical therapist. She taught me new ways to manage the daily activities of living, all without bending my spine. I learned how to pick things up off the floor, load and unload the clothes washer, get into and out of bed by rolling, putting on my clothes, and tying my shoes while keeping my back and neck perfectly straight.

But the ability to perform my daily activities was further restricted by my left arm hanging in a sling due to my broken left clavicle. I could use only one good arm to try to put on clothes and shoes, cook, eat, and wash dishes, which made everything more difficult and time-consuming.

Taking care of my basic daily activities now consumed most of the day. Eating breakfast, showering, dressing, brushing my teeth, and doing something with my hair took up half of the morning now. Next, I went for a walk and by the time I got back, it was time for lunch. After that, I usually took a nap.[36] After a nap, I found time to keep up on paperwork: bills, bills, and more bills. Then another walk in the late afternoon, followed by dinner and a couple of hours relaxing in the evening. By 8 PM I was more than ready for a night of sleep.

Once again, I felt empathy for anyone struggling with mobility issues. Those of us with normal mobility take the daily chores for granted, but when your mobility is impaired, nothing is easy or quick anymore.

At my six-week checkups with my surgeons, I was very disappointed to learn that I had no bone healing at all. Nothing. My doctors expressed that they didn't feel terribly concerned, but I was. I had my heart set on the idea that my bones would be fully healed in two months and my back fusion by six months. Reality was rearing its not-so-pretty head. I felt frustration again that my body wasn't progressing as I thought it should. My life should be back to almost-normal by now, shouldn't it?

But I did make a huge leap of progress on that visit: my surgeon cleared me to remove both my neck brace and body cast. Yippie! My muscles and other soft tissues would recover more quickly if the brace

---

36 One of the things that my brain injury required in order to heal was a lot of time sleeping. I could not go a day without a nap of some kind, and some days I required two. I'd reach a point during the day where my brain would just stop functioning and then I knew it was time for sleep. For about ten months after my accident, daily naps were absolutely necessary. In some ways it was like being a child again.

and body cast were removed. I would still need to work with a physical therapist to regain my strength and my ability to drive a car again, but I didn't need my exoskeleton anymore.

My left collarbone still felt tender to the touch at six weeks, even though it didn't hurt me to move it. While I was now cleared to resume activity with that arm, it would continue to feel weak for many months.

At ten months, the healing of my bones progressed at a snail's pace. By November of 2014, the only bones that have healed fully are those in my ribs. My collarbone and most of the broken vertebrae, as well as my fusion, have not knit together fully. It frustrates me occasionally to continue to feel like a broken doll. I continue to exercise, eat healthy foods, and do moderate weightlifting, but at this point, I am still simply trusting that my bones will heal in time.

The months have worked to ease the pain in my back, although it flares up after long periods of sitting. Hiking, walking, some off-road cycling (on easy bike paths), and weight-lifting are my main forms of exercise right now. I'm still cautious about getting back on a road bike or participating in activities such as downhill skiing that have a high risk of injury. I know that, in time, I'll be back doing most of the things I've loved for most of my life. For now, though, caution is my rule of the day.

MIND

The most surprising aspect of my recovery has been the snail's pace of my brain healing. The crash caused me to suffer a traumatic brain injury (TBI) even though I wore my helmet.[37] My brain trauma concerned my primary care doctor more than anything else I'd endured. Based on the scans and my initial impairments, he predicted that it would take at least 12-18 months, and possibly 24 or more, for my brain to heal. Only after that would we know which impairments would be permanent.

---

37 There is no doubt that if I had not worn a helmet, I would have died at the scene from brain trauma. Please, if you or your loved ones ride a bike, wear a helmet!

Massive headaches a few times a week, some irritability, and sleepiness challenged me. These symptoms are very common after a brain injury, but my doctor assured me they would fade away within about three months. It turns out that he was right — within six weeks, the headaches tapered off. By three months the irritability had disappeared, and the sleepiness continued until about six months post-accident.

But it was the longer-term effects that concerned me. These included balance problems, memory loss, word-finding difficulties, and speech impediments. Bouts of feeling unable to balance came several times a week. They lasted just a few seconds but were nerve-wracking enough that I needed to walk with a companion close by in order to feel safe.

For the first nine months, memory loss frustrated me daily. I struggled with remembering the names of friends who I had known for years. Even face-to-face, I stumbled to put names with faces. On my first day back in the office (more than three months post-accident), several of my coworkers greeted me. It horrified me that I couldn't pull any of their names from my memory. These were people whom I'd known for 18 months and whose faces I recognized, but I just could not remember their names. My heart broke after several of these attempted greetings. I felt terrible, ran back to my office, shut the door, and cried. I felt as though my mind had betrayed me and I worried that my memory would be forever impaired. I didn't want to go through life unable to remember the names of my friends.

Another troubling symptom I noticed after my accident was an occasional inability to speak coherently. I often struggled to find the right words for the concepts I attempted to verbalize. In my mind's eye, I could see pictures of what I wanted to say but I just couldn't put a word to that picture in a spoken sentence. Another related problem that frustrated me was jumbling my words into an incoherent mess when I tried to speak. When in a conversation, at times I'd know the correct words but speak them in a massive, muddled mess. The person to whom I spoke would often give me a confused look and I'd have to restart the sentence. I felt embarrassed when this happened and would explain that I was recovering from a brain injury. Everyone was gracious about this and by nine months after my accident, the muddled word problem seems to have disappeared. I continue my struggle with word-finding, though.

My ability to write even simple computer programs and think analytically seemed to have vanished with my memory. Both comprised the major part of my career for the last 15 years and now I struggled with them. I relied heavily on my coworkers for help every day but by late May of 2014, I knew things weren't improving. One day I came in to the office, sat down at my computer to create a simple programming tutorial for our corporate blog, and my mind just could not process the task. I simply stared at my computer screen, unable to formulate how to even outline the task, let alone start programming.

This used to be easy!

My frustration level rose as I realized I couldn't remember any of the syntax of our programming language. I felt utterly useless, and I began to feel a sense of deep compassion and some understanding of what other TBI patients suffered. My injuries were small in comparison to some I'd heard about. I could still function pretty well on a daily basis, even though I struggled in certain areas. But I somehow felt *different* now.

A large part of who I thought I was no longer existed.

I wept, and grieved the woman who I thought had somehow perished in that crash. I knew then I'd have to find another way to make a living, at least for the short term.

My brain injury did have some benefits. My creativity increased exponentially and I found that I was able to paint more effectively and efficiently than ever before. Ideas for new paintings came at such a fast clip that I didn't have enough time to paint them all.

Ideas for creative writing projects flowed easily, too. While I struggled with the practice of writing (I still do), I felt compelled to put my words out there on the blogsphere and eventually into this book.

I saw that I now had an opportunity to do something I'd wanted to do for years. It was time for me to follow my heart's calling and make a leap of faith into the unknown. I left my job in late May of 2014 to pursue an independent career as a writer and artist.

This was a scary step for the old me, but one that was long overdue.

CHAPTER 19

My Life Changes

My life continues to evolve as a result of the accident and the near-death experience with which I was blessed. I will doubtless continue processing all of the experiences and information for the remainder of my time on Earth. This one lifetime isn't even close to long enough to understand all of the mystery that is Spirit.

Even though in human terms I was in Heaven for only a brief stay, I've found re-entry into society challenging at times. I miss the profound feeling of love that permeated Heaven, and the strong, tangible connection to Spirit. When I struggle with this today, I simply go on a walk in the sunshine and look for evidence of love. It works. I come back refreshed, renewed, and ready to continue on with my day.

On the flip side, I can now more easily *sense* the Spirit and love all around me. It's easier now for me to notice that light inside everyone, even people who aren't behaving from a loving place in that particular moment. That light is there, though, and I'm grateful to be able to sense it.

Something that still takes me by surprise is that I'm much more emotional now. I seem to be more strongly connected to feelings than ever before, mine and others'. I allow myself to cry when strong feelings overwhelm me. Previously, I viewed crying as a sign of weakness and denied it to myself as an emotional outlet. Now I find myself tearing up at seeing a beautiful demonstration of love, such as a new mother cradling her baby on their first walk in the park together. I cry too when I feel deeply and profoundly grateful for what I have, and for the opportunities I've been given. Overall, I'm more heart-centered, more intuitive, and more creative.

As you might be able to guess, my fear of death is gone. I do still deal with fears or concerns from time to time, but none of them have anything to do with death. While I'm not looking to revisit Heaven any time soon, I no longer feel fear when thinking about the eventual end of my life.

I live more from a space of gratitude and love now. Snags come along and I have to ground or center myself to continue on. The hurts of the past occasionally haunt me, and in those moments I struggle to return to a place of love. My one saving grace is practicing gratitude on a daily basis, and going on the "love walks" I mentioned earlier in the book. The practice of gratitude grounds me in the here and now, and those "love walks" force me to realize that the world is much bigger than just me.

Overall, I *am* happier these days. I still experience times where things aren't so good and my outlook isn't terribly rosy, but they are few and far between now. But then again, this is just a part of life for most of us.

Some friends have left my life while new ones continue to come in. I mourn the passage of unhealthy friendships and celebrate the new opportunities for connection that come regularly these days.

Longtime friends have noted a change in my energy and in the ways I interact with them. They say I am more peaceful, centered, and calm now, and that I seem to act from a place of peace. I can't really speak to this except to say that I'm still *me*. What they may be sensing is my new willingness to take calculated risks, to live from the heart, and to live the life that *feels* right for me. I believe that when you are truly living your life in harmony with who you are, your energy shifts into something positive and upbeat most of the time.

While my brain's functioning has now returned to normal, one odd change in my physical body seems set. I can no longer tolerate certain things that I used to consume occasionally, especially sugars and alcohol. The old me enjoyed a glass of wine occasionally, but today, even a few sips will cause me to feel ill for much of the next day. This doesn't really bother me. It's more of a curiosity that I can't explain.

One thing that truly surprised me is the change in my art, specifically in my preferred subject matter. In the spring of 2014, I followed an intuition to photograph and paint horses. The horses that tugged on my heart initially were the wild horses of the Wyoming and Colorado Bureau of Land Management (BLM) lands. Their apparent freedom, exuberance, stamina, and courageous living inspired me in a way that defies explanation. Perhaps they were simply an outward symbol of the kinds of energies I wanted to bring into my life: intuitive, free, heart-centered, beautiful, athletic, graceful. Whatever the reason, the wild horses began the process of opening my heart to life again.

An intuition to photograph and paint Spanish Colonial Horses (Spanish Mustangs, Andalusians, Paso Finos, etc.) came to me later that summer. Their connection to the deep history of our human cultures captivated me. Their graceful movement, hardiness, strength, and stamina encouraged me in my healing process. Even more incredible is how their beauty sometimes made me cry from gratitude from the depths of my being. Just being able to see one of these beauties go through its gaits was magical. Their steps flowed, and they inspired me in my quest to regain my mobility.

It might not come as a surprise, then, that in May of 2014, I made a conscious decision to live more from my heart and intuition rather than making all of my choices solely from my brain. I still allow my critical thinking abilities to weigh in, but unless I see some dire outcome, I take the advice of my heart and intuition. While it feels like a more graceful, harmonious way of living, it hasn't always been an easy road to walk.

I've found that listening to what my heart and intuition say can make my mind very uncomfortable. The heart wants me to take risks that my mind might find terrifying; it wants me to take a chance to create the life I've always dreamed of. And the intuition works from a place of quick decisions that seem to defy logic or reasoning — the antithesis of how my brain has functioned. But the mind wants plans, certainties, and no risk. It's a tough balance; one that I readjust every day.

I still don't know what lies in front of me, but I'm excited to see where this new path in a life of love leads.

CHAPTER 20

A New Job

About three weeks after I came home, I woke up in the middle of the night with an overwhelming urge to finish writing down everything my Guide told me. I now had full memory — those parts that were fuzzy suddenly came back. I realized that if I didn't write it all down, everything might evaporate from my mind. I quickly jotted down the main points, not really paying too much attention to what came from my pen. The information flowed effortlessly. I wrote for over an hour. When I felt as though I captured enough for the moment, I put my notes away and fell asleep again.

The next morning I glanced at them and couldn't believe what I'd written. More accurately, I couldn't recall having generated the words I saw in front of me, even though I do remember writing. It was as if I had taken dictation, not really aware of what I heard and wrote. As I read the notes aloud to my sister, a wave of emotion rose up out of my core and overwhelmed me. I sobbed. The beauty and love that were bound up in what my Guide had taught me suddenly hit me full force. It overwhelmed my human emotions. I felt a little tendril of love from my Guide touch me again and I began to cry. My sister Jennifer was with me at the time and she simply put her arms around me in support and allowed me to let the emotion flow through and out.

It seemed that my new job had just started.

Over the next few weeks, I continued to write. I felt the urge to put pen to paper more strongly as I woke in the morning. Sometimes I'd take my notebook out in nature, often to a stream or a lake, and write for hours.

At other times I would remember the waves of love, joy, and peace intermixed with visuals of the messages in my mind. I understand now these were concepts my Guide wanted us to know but didn't know how to express in words. Some days the process of writing exhausted my physical body, but my emotions and spirit always felt energized and lightened by the work.

For the first time ever in my life, I wanted to read the words of many of the world's great spiritual teachers, including the New Testament. I also felt the need to learn more about the life of Lao Tsu, the Buddha, St. Francis, and many others, but particularly Jesus. I'd spent most of my adult life avoiding the New Testament, even though I thought Jesus was a pretty cool guy who tried to teach us us many amazing things.

Eventually, I tried to return to church and attend other spiritual gatherings. I wasn't sure that going into a building to worship with others would be very helpful or moving. In fact, I kind of balked at the concept of *worship*. Prayer or meditation I could understand and support, but there was something about the concept of *worship* that felt vaguely unempowering. I was the kind of person who preferred to be active in my own enlightenment and self-improvement. I also thought that being in a church would be just as good as being alone and praying. Wouldn't Spirit be able to hear me better when I was alone, anyway? But then I remembered one of the things my Guide wanted me to do: to seek out and join with a community whenever possible. Humans were meant to be together, to connect with others whether in a church, a sports team, an art group, or just hanging out with friends. Our minds and emotions are better in a team.

I attended a church service or two close to my home. My first time visiting one of them reinforced my new job. The sermon was the start of a series about living a mission given to us from Spirit.

Tears ran down my cheeks for the entire hour.

The minister spoke about being called to serve, not being afraid to take a stand and do good work for others. He talked about how Jesus was called to serve, how he healed and helped others, and taught that we can do just as he did.

I began to understand then just how other profoundly spiritual people have served humanity: Mother Teresa in India, St. Francis in Europe, the Buddha in Asia, The Dalai Lama, and many more. They and many others chose to be of service to others, even if in a small way.

I couldn't wait to sit at my desk and continue the work: to put into words the information I'd been given.

I still remember every detail of the crash, being in the hospital, and the recovery process. Friends have said they thought remembering everything would be too traumatic. They contend that they would want to have amnesia if it happened to them. While I didn't have a choice in whether I remembered or not, I now see those memories as a blessing.

Why?

They allowed me a first glimpse into the nature of my existence on Earth, of the reality of my spirituality, and that I have nothing to fear in dying.

More important than the memories of the accident are the ones from the Guide I met, and the information she passed on to me. I remember the love, the beauty, peace, harmony, and the loving presence that suffused everything there. I carry it with me still. It might get a little lost in the humanness of daily life, but it's there when I consciously choose to call on it.

That little bit of Heaven is as real to me as sitting here at this computer, typing. Actually, it's more real.

That place, whatever you choose to call it, is our true home. It is where our souls ultimately belong. There, we are loved beyond all reasoning. We are connected to each other in ways we can't conceive of here on Earth. Spirit's love suffuses us in ways that would cripple our human brains to try to understand.

Whether you choose to believe in Heaven or not, spiritual love is there for you all of the time. If what I experienced was nothing more than encountering the depths and truths of my own humanity, the knowledge and insights I gained is worth the pain I endured. But in my own internal wisdom, I believe and trust that my experience was somehow more than that. I did come face-to-face with my inner truths, but I think I touched on something more profound and mysterious.

Do I know for sure what comes after this life?

No.

As a scientist, I can only say that I experienced something profound and mysterious that has changed my life forever. While I have a hint of what's to come, and got a glimpse of something profoundly spiritual, I can't explain it in scientific terms. It's simply mysterious and awe-inspiring, and I'm OK leaving at that.

This book and my speaking engagements are my attempt to pass on what I learned from my time with my Guide. I hope that some part of the information resonates with you and brings you comfort, joy, and peace.

CHAPTER 21

Why Me?

W HY WAS I CHOSEN? O UT of the thousands of people who die every day in the USA, why was I given a chance to experience something so mysterious and profound, gain some insights, and then come back for another chance? More importantly, why was I gifted with information such as that which is in this book?

I'm not a minister, saint, guru, or spiritual leader, nor do I intend to become any of these things. In fact, before this accident I didn't admit to the existence of anything other than this physical reality around us. I considered myself an agnostic scientist at best: open to the possibility that there might be something out there, but waiting to see proof of its existence.

In most ways, though, I'm relatively normal just like most people reading this book. I've made some huge blunders in my life and done some good things too. I've reacted in anger, felt sadness, loved and lost, grieved, called off relationships, divorced, and pretty much everything else that comes with living a life today.

I'm nothing out of the ordinary, really.

That simple statement may hold the explanation.

I'm normal. I'm pretty much like you. On any other day it might not have been me hit by that car and thrown down the rabbit's hole of life changes — it could have been you.

The only difference between me and most of you reading this may be that I had years of training and practice as a scientist, and technical communicator. I'm skilled at many forms of communication and wasn't too daunted to take on the challenge of bringing this book into existence.

But then again, perhaps the best answer I can come up with to the original question is: "Because God asked me to."

CHAPTER 22

What's in it for You?

As I CONTINUE TO PROCESS everything that happened during my experience, I understand that it will take me a lifetime to even come close to integrating it into my life. The amount of information my Guide gave me is staggering. Given that, what are some of the most important things for you to take away from all of this?

For anyone reading this book, I think that answer will ultimately be an individual one. I can't tell you what's important for you to learn in your life, just as you can't say what's important for me in mine. But some of the things I learned bear particular importance to my Guide so I'll stress those in this chapter. Before I do that, though, let's review the messages again.

The Messages
The Messages are short and deceptively simple:

1. We are not on Earth to simply learn, but to love
2. You are a miracle — treat yourself like one
3. This Earth and the universe are miracles
4. Each one of us is more powerful than we can imagine
5. Each one of us, all of Creation, is a part of Spirit
6. Allow, let go, let Spirit work in your life
7. Show love to others by allowing them to show love

8. Learn to listen to your heart
9. We are never alone
10. Our most powerful tool for living is our power of choice
11. You have one chance at life as You — live it fully
12. Live and feel your gratitude as much as possible

Remember, the wisdom of these messages is our birthright. We may have forgotten some of them or maybe didn't realize their importance but we're being given a chance to bring them back into our consciousness in order to live better lives here, now, on this Earth.

TAKEAWAYS

One or more of the messages themselves will likely be your biggest takeaway from this book, but there are several other items whose importance became apparent to me during the months after my accident:

1. Work to create your version of Heaven on Earth.
2. Start by learning to love yourself.
3. Community is extremely important.
4. Play, have fun, live in joy and love.

Spirit wants us to live this life as fully and lovingly as possible. Don't stay mired in misery while you wait for some future promise of Heaven. This life you have is your chance to create a bit of Heaven here on Earth, right now. Try to make your own life more heavenly by, in part, using these messages. See if you can improve your own life and the lives of your family members even a little bit.

How should you start? One good way is learning to love yourself for the miracle that you are. You have unique gifts, abilities, thoughts, opinions, and an energy that this world needs. Too many of us dislike or even hate ourselves, which can lead to a host of issues in our lives. Start improving your life by beginning to recognize your glorious, miraculous nature. No, you're not perfect, nor is anyone else. But you are beautiful, creative, and amazing just as you are. See Spirit's presence in you. Once you start seeing, loving, and accepting yourself as a spiritual being, your fears will begin to melt away and you'll be open to making changes that will improve your life further. But it all starts with extending love to yourself. If you find it difficult to extend love to yourself, try extending love and compassion to others, instead, then circle around and work on self-love again.

Cultivating a community around you is essential for living a full, joyous life. We all need help at some time in our lives but without a community of friends or family around us, we may not have that support when we need it most. Additionally, humans are social creatures who need the kind of close interactions that communities provide in order to feel loved, valued, and truly connected to the world around us.

But life shouldn't be all seriousness and learning and striving to be better. We're here to enjoy life as much as we can. Laugh. Dance. Ski. Swim. Watch the sun set. Dip your toes in the ocean. Play with your kids. Enjoy your pets. Gaze in awe at mountains. Fall in love. Help a friend. Open your heart and sing your gratitude to Spirit for this glorious life you've been given.

CHAPTER 23

In Closing

THE CONTENT OF THIS BOOK continues to help me every day. Even after its completion and all of the hours spent writing and rewriting this material, I'm still only human. I'm not perfect and continue to face challenges, some related to the accident and some not. I sometimes struggle with relationships, communication, and being vulnerable. I can feel hurt, angry, or sad. Overall, though, my life is much happier, more contented, and feels more blessed than at any other time. This book continues to remind me of what truly is important in these precious decades that I have on Earth.

Life shouldn't be all seriousness, struggle, and self-improvement though. One of the things I took away from my experience is to enjoy my days on Earth as much as I can. I hope you do, too.

Do what you love to the best of your abilities. This is one of the ingredients for an inspired life.

Listen to the callings of your heart, for in it is the key to happiness and fulfillment. It's one of God's way of speaking directly to you.

Know that there is more than just this life, that Spirit is there for us any time, and our life on Earth is precious and wonderful.

My hope is that this book will help you live a fulfilled life complete with happiness, joy, and love.

The Power of Two

Thank you for allowing me to share my experience with you.

My near-death experience, and the messages I received in Heaven, continue to have a huge impact on my life. It's part of my calling to spread Heaven's message of love to all who want to hear it — you can help by telling others about this book or my blog.

If you enjoyed reading this book, I graciously ask that you tell at least two friends about it.

Peace,

Nancy Rynes

AwakeningsFromTheLight.com

TheSpiritWay.BlogSpot.com

Part Four

Appendices

A)
What Did Death Feel Like?

―⚉―

As I CONTINUED TO WORK on writing this book and thinking about the accident, one thing continued to surprise me: how easy it was for my body to die. The way I mean "easy" is that it didn't seem as traumatic as I always assumed an accidental death would be. It's a strange thing to be given a clear glimpse of death, then come back to ponder it and share the experience. It just doesn't happen that often, and certainly not with people I know. My feeling is now that if I share what I experienced as I approached death, it just might help others who are dealing with the loss of a loved one or working through their own fears of mortality.

Like most of us, I used to contemplate my own death from time to time and always came up against fears: that dying would be painful, terrifying, difficult, or emotionally wrenching. And what came after death? The thought of my consciousness ending, just ceasing to function and slipping into darkness, scared me too. That dark *nothingness* at the end of life terrified me the most. The more years I had under my belt, the more I grew to fear the inevitability of life ending. Like so many people, my coping mechanism became avoiding the thought of death altogether. If I didn't think about it, it wouldn't happen, right? It was a problem that was bigger and darker than I could face.

It surprised me, then, that during my accident, from the moment of impact until after the paramedics arrived, I literally felt no physical pain and in fact felt very little physical sensation anywhere in my body. It felt as though my entire body was numbed by a painkiller. I would have expected to be in unspeakable pain from the moment the truck impacted me, but that wasn't the case. I physically felt almost nothing during those minutes, or at least I had no sensation of pain. While I knew at the time that the truck had hit me, I really didn't register the physical feeling of its impact on my body or the subsequent trauma of the crash itself.

It's very strange to my mind even today, and I can't explain it.

Would everyone going through a trauma like mine be immune to pain and physical sensation? I have no idea. I can only relate what I experienced. I do hope that this is the case, though.

Knowing how my accident felt to my body makes me a bit calmer and less grief-stricken about the traumatic death of my oldest sister in a car accident years ago. I hope that her final moments were devoid of pain. After my experience, I suspect they were.

It may be that this lack of pain was a result of my body's own painkillers (endorphins) kicking in to high gear. However, besides removing the pain, whatever process that took place also seemed to calm my mind. While I did feel a mild level of fear, it wasn't as all-consuming as I might expect. The fear felt somewhat detached, as if I was listening to thoughts from someone else. The fear was mine, while at the same time, not quite mine. Even more interesting to me now, the fear felt easily manageable. My brain seemed to put that fear into a little compartment separate from the rest of my thoughts. Panic didn't overtake me. My thinking seemed pretty clear: "I wonder how my family will react," "Hold on to that license plate," "Hold on to that axle," "Get up and run."

Pain and panic didn't really kick in until after the paramedics arrived and began to prepare me for transport to the ER.

As my consciousness effortlessly split into the "watcher-me" and the "human-me" during the crash, in a strange way all felt *right* somehow, even though I still can't explain this feeling of *rightness*.

The split happened without effort. One microsecond I was in my human body and in the next my consciousness existed in two places, experiencing the accident from separate vantage points. I felt no anxiety about this split. It seemed natural. The watcher-me (the one outside of my body) felt a little sad I was experiencing this trauma, but she also knew with a grand knowing that everything would be A-OK. That even though the crash was traumatic, I was experiencing something necessary for me to experience, and all was fine.

The watcher-me felt like the real me: a timeless me, the part of my existence that doesn't die. Perhaps some might call it my soul. Thanks to this accident I know that it really does exist, that we aren't just humans, and that there is more to life and living than this beautiful embodiment of biology that we call our bodies.

I now understand that we are not simply collections of skills, knowledge, or activities. There is a core *something* that is deeper, more universal, much older, and wiser. My soul is not the scared animal consciousness stuck in a battered body being dragged under a truck. It is that one who watched, the one who observed it all. My soul experienced some gentle sadness but at the same time knew that *this was as it had to be in this moment*. The real me is the one who stayed calm and knew that everything I experienced through those weeks had a purpose, and that I would be OK.

My near-death experience in surgery also felt effortless and *right*. One second I was drifting off from the anesthesia and in the next, bright light, hills, trees, and warm breezes surrounded me. That place was so captivating and so much my true home that I didn't want to leave. The process of going there was not painful, traumatic, or terrifying. It was easy. It was *right*.

This effortless split of my higher consciousness from my body helps me to understand the process of death a little better too. In my case it wasn't painful or terrifying. Experiencing what I believe is a glimpse into the realm of mystery removed my fear of death. I no longer dread it. I know it's coming, though, and will choose to truly live my life fully and with passion from here on out.

B)
The Others

In a few places in this book, I mention that my Guide was not alone in speaking to me and that she was a messenger for many others. Before I packaged this information together into a book, readers of my blog often asked about these other entities. The most common thing people wanted to know was: who are they?

I asked my guide the same question. I'll share their answer with you now, in their own words:

We are those who have lived before and gone on. We are also those yet to be born into your world, and some who may never be born. We are here in love, loving you, helping you, guiding you as best as we can.

We are also those who you might call angels, saints, apostles, disciples, and teachers. And of course, "we" also and most importantly, includes Spirit. For it is the love that emanates from Spirit into all of us that makes this happen. That love forms the basic structure of all of this — your world and this realm where we exist. This love and creative force binds us all together, runs through all of us, and connects us to each other. Spirit is a part of each one of us, and each one of us is a part of Spirit.

We love you so much and we can't wait for you to return home, to be here with us. But know that where you are now is a magical place. You have things we cannot have — experiences that are tangible and reinforce the spiritual because of the physical place you live in. You can help create the miracle of a baby, you can look into that baby's face after giving birth and experience that profound human love a parent has for a child. You can also look into that child's eyes and see divinity right there in front of you, all innocence, trust, and love. Soak it in. Allow that experience of unimaginable, profound love to flow through you and take over, to wash through your heart, and soften your spirit.

You can also experience the joys of romantic love. You can connect with another human so deeply that all else becomes secondary. You can grow a bond that can last a lifetime. And this bond is a microcosm of the love the Divine feels for all of us. In experiencing this deep, profound loving of another human, you can live inside and experience a portion of spiritual love.

But at the same time, where you are [Earth] can hinder your feelings and expression of love. We here experience Spirit's love and thoughts firsthand, unencumbered.

Where you are, it can be hard to hear Spirit's voice in your heart. It can be hard to feel that love on a daily basis. It can be difficult to see miracles. You have all of the joys and pleasures of Earth but you also have the distractions that can make it hard to hear and feel spiritual love in your life.

And so we choose to pass some of these messages on to you through this writer. She was asked to serve in this way. Know that these words are not all hers — we passed the messages along to her in the same way that Spirit passed them along to us.

We send them to you because some of you may need or want to read more experiences of Divine that happen today. You may need to read about ideas in ways that seem more directly pertinent to your life, or simply read concepts in a different way for them to make sense.

These teachings are here for you, when you need them.

C)

Reading List

───❦───

A few books that I find uplifting and inspirational:

    The Dalai Lama: *The Universe in a Single Atom*
    Collette, Amy: *The Gratitude Connection*
    Dyer, Dr. Wayne: *Inspiration: Your Ultimate Calling*
    Elliott, Ken: *Manifesting 1-2-3*
    Frankl, Viktor: *Man's Search for Meaning*
    Hanh, Thich Nhat: *Going Home: Jesus and Buddha as Brothers*
    Hanh, Thich Nhat: *The World We Have*
    Ruiz, don Miguel: *The Four Agreements*

Information on physical and mental health:

    Amen, Dr. Daniel: the *Change Your Brain...* series is especially helpful
    Cordain, Dr. Loren: *The Paleo Diet*
    Sisson, Mark: *The Primal Blueprint*
    Weil, Dr. Andrew: *Spontaneous Happiness*
    Weil, Dr. Andrew: *8 Weeks to Optimum Health*

About the Author

Nancy Rynes was born and raised on a small farm near Woodstock, Illinois. She is a writer and artist who currently resides near Boulder, Colorado.

Rynes spent most of her life as a scientist and skeptic. She earned a BSc in geology from Northern Illinois University, completing her Masters level coursework at the University of Colorado, Boulder. She also has a fine arts education from the American Academy of Art in Chicago.

Rynes has experience as an archeological artist, geologist, data analyst, and field technician for wildlife biology projects. From 1994 on, she has worked as a science and technical writer in aerospace, healthcare, and software engineering.

Born Roman Catholic, Rynes became an atheist, and later an agnostic, beginning in her late teens. Since her near-death experience, she has returned to a more spiritual and creative life based on the wisdom she learned in Heaven.

Nancy's Programs

AWAKENINGS FROM THE LIGHT

As the author of *Awakenings from the Light,* Nancy speaks about the depth of love and connection to Spirit that is our birthright. In fun, positive, and engaging talks and seminars, she shares her experiences while in Heaven, and how we can use that information to enhance both our personal and professional lives. Available in several formats.

YOUR CREATIVE VISION — FINDING AND NURTURING YOUR MUSE

"Your Creative Vision" expands on the creativity message found in *Awakenings from the Light* and teaches artists of all kinds a process for developing and nurturing their own signature style.

For more information or to schedule any of these programs, please see:

NancyRynes.com

Made in the USA
Columbia, SC
15 July 2024